D0248202

# The Charity Trustee's Handbook

## 2nd edition

Mike Eastwood

# DIRECTORY OF SOCIAL CHANGE

Published by
Directory of Social Change
24 Stephenson Way
London NWI 2DP
Tel: 08450 77 77 07; Fax: 020 73914804
email: publications@dsc.org.uk
www.dsc.org.uk
from whom further copies and a full books catalogue are available.

Directory of Social Change Northern Office
Federation House, Hope Street, Liverpool LI 9BW
Policy and Research 0151 708 0136; email: research@dsc.org.uk

Directory of Social Change is a Registered Charity no. 800517

First published 2001
Reprinted 2003, 2005 and 2007
Second edition 2010
Reprinted 2011

Copyright © Directory of Social Change 2001, 2010

The moral right of the author has been asserted in accordance with the
Copyright, Designs and Patents Act 1988

All rights reserved. **No part of this book may be stored in a
retrieval system or reproduced in any form whatsoever without
prior permission in writing from the publisher – apart from the
Checklists on pages 97–110 © Sandy Adirondack, which may be
photocopied.** This book is sold subject to the condition that it shall not,
by way of trade or otherwise, be lent, re-sold, hired out or otherwise
circulated without the publisher's prior permission in any form of binding or
cover other than that in which it is published, and without a similar condition
including this condition being imposed on the subsequent purchaser.

ISBN 978 1 906294 65 6

**British Library Cataloguing in Publication Data**
A catalogue record for this book is available from the British Library

Cover design by Kate Bass
Original text design by Sarah Nicholson
Typeset by Marlinzo Services, Frome
Printed and bound by Page Bros, Norwich

MIX
Paper from
responsible sources
FSC® C023114
www.fsc.org

# Contents

**About the series**                                        v

**Preface**                                                 vi

**Foreword**                                                vii

**About the author**                                        viii

**Acknowledgements**                                        viii

**About the Directory of Social Change**                    ix

PART ONE
**What makes a good trustee?**                              I

I    What is a trustee?                                      3

2    Who can be a trustee?                                   I I

3    Why be a trustee?                                       I5

4    Why refuse to be a trustee?                             I7

5    How long should you remain a trustee?                   I9

PART TWO
**Key roles of trustees**                                   2I

6    The role of the management committee                    23

7    Understanding your organisation                         29

8    Understanding your staff and volunteers                 4I

9    Understanding your finances                             49

I0   Getting the resources                                   57

I I  Being accountable                                       67

PART THREE
**Getting the work done**                                   73

I2   Organising your meetings                                75

I3   Special roles on the management
     committee                                               8I

I4   Delegation                                              85

**PART FOUR**
**Getting the most out of being a trustee**            91

15   Pulling it all together                                  93

**Checklists**                                                97

1    The legal and management framework        98

2    Governance                                           100

3    Information, communication and decision
     making                                               102

4    Employment and volunteers                     103

5    Finance                                              106

6    Personal effectiveness                          109

**Dealing with numbers**                              111

     Reading management accounts               112

     Reading annual accounts                        118

**Useful addresses**                                    121

**Publications**                                          127

**Index**                                                 132

# About the series

This series of key guides is designed for people involved with not-for-profit organisations of any size, no matter how you define your organisation: voluntary, community, non-governmental or social enterprise. All the titles offer practical, comprehensive, yet accessible advice to enable readers to get the most out of their roles and responsibilities.

## Other titles in the series

Also available in this series:

*Charitable Status*, Julian Blake, 2008

*The Charity Treasurer's Handbook*, Gareth G. Morgan, 2010

*Effective Fundraising*, Luke Fitzherbert, 2004

*Minute Taking*, Paul Ticher and Lee Comer, 2012

For further information, please contact the Directory of Social Change (see page ix for details).

# Preface

There are well over a million people currently serving as charity trustees in the UK. They range from people sitting on trustee boards of household-name charities, such as Oxfam and the National Trust, to members of the management committees of small, local charities operating in a single village or parish. They include members of church councils, some housing associations, parent–teacher associations and community groups, and even some school governors.

This is a book for those who are, or are thinking of becoming, a charity trustee. It doesn't aim to tell you everything; rather, it aims to give you enough information to decide whether you should become a trustee or, if you are already one, some ideas on how to make your trusteeship more rewarding. Although it refers particularly to charities, it will also be useful for committee members of other community and voluntary organisations that are not registered charities.

It can be read straight through from start to finish. However, you can also use it as a basic reference guide and dip into it to help you with particular issues or concerns.

Being a trustee is, or should be, fulfilling. You are using your skills to help an organisation that you believe in to change things for the better. Sometimes this can be frustrating; often it can be challenging; occasionally you will want to give the whole thing up. However, fundamentally you should derive a lot of personal satisfaction from seeing something you are committed to flourish and develop.

Good luck!


Mike Eastwood

# Foreword

We have all seen newspaper features entitled '100 films to watch before you die', or 'top 10 essential reads'. I am always doubtful about how must-read something is, or whether I really will feel incomplete if I don't watch all those films before my time is up.

Not everything in life really is must-see, must-do, or must-read. But there are many activities that do at least demand a thorough read of a how-to or how-not-to guide or set of instructions before we start them. You don't build an IKEA bookshelf without instructions, or set out on a long journey without a satnav or directions to stop you getting lost.

So neither, surely, would you dream of setting off as a charity trustee without the proper directions or instructions to make sure you don't get 'lost' or end up creating something, i.e. your charity, in completely the wrong way.

I would, of course, always recommend that charity trustees can avoid the pitfalls by studiously reading Charity Commission guidance and publications. But equally, having something which includes case studies and quotes, and useful practical suggestions is helpful alongside the dos and don'ts of charity law and good practice.

*The Charity Trustee's Handbook* is a very readable and practical guide that provides a positive focus on the skills and experience that you as a trustee can bring, as well as the rewarding experience that trusteeship can be for you. Advice on how to make sure your trustee meetings are dynamic and exciting rather than tedious and unfulfilling will be very welcome, as will the handy checklists and guidance to help demystify charity accounts. I hope that you find this 'satnav' for trusteeship a valuable tool and a true must-read publication.

Andrew Hind
Chief Executive
Charity Commission

# About the author

Mike Eastwood is currently Diocesan Secretary in the diocese of Liverpool and Director of Operations for Liverpool Cathedral. He is also a trustee of Merseyside Community Foundation and the Church Urban Fund.

Mike was chief executive of the Directory of Social Change from 1995 to 2001, chair of trustees for the National Association for Voluntary and Community Action, a member of the Advisory Council to the Charities Aid Foundation and a trustee for Liverpool Council for Social Service.

Mike is author of two of DSC's publications: *The Charity Trustee's Handbook* and *Writing Better Fundraising Applications*.

# Acknowledgements

The author and publishers would like to thank Tim Cook, Ruth Froggatt, Linda Laurance, Neal Green and Sarah Miller at the Charity Commission and Lucy Swanson for their input at different stages of this book's and the last edition's preparation. Their knowledge, experience and insights have been invaluable.

Thanks, too, to Sandy Adirondack for the helpful checklists at the back of the book.

And thanks to the many trustees and management committee members who have shared their experiences with us.

# About the Directory of Social Change

DSC has a vision of an independent voluntary sector at the heart of social change. The activities of independent charities, voluntary organisations and community groups are fundamental to achieve social change. We exist to help these organisations and the people who support them to achieve their goals.

We do this by:

- providing practical tools that organisations and activists need, including online and printed publications, training courses, and conferences on a huge range of topics

- acting as a 'concerned citizen' in public policy debates, often on behalf of smaller charities, voluntary organisations and community groups

- leading campaigns and stimulating debate on key policy issues that affect those groups

- carrying out research and providing information to influence policymakers.

DSC is the leading provider of information and training for the voluntary sector and publishes an extensive range of guides and handbooks covering subjects such as fundraising, management, communication, finance and law. We have a range of subscription-based websites containing a wealth of information on funding from trusts, companies and government sources. We run more than 300 training courses each year, including bespoke in-house training provided at the client's location. DSC conferences, many of which run on an annual basis, include the Charity Management Conference, the Charity Accountants' Conference and the Charity Law Conference. DSC's major annual event is Charityfair, which provides low-cost training on a wide variety of subjects.

For details of all our activities, and to order publications and book courses, go to www.dsc.org.uk, call 08450 777707 or email publications@dsc.org.uk

# PART **ONE**

# What makes a good trustee?

# 1 What is a trustee?

This is not a book mainly about charity law, nor about the details of your legal responsibilities and liabilities. Rather, it aims to be a practical guide about how to operate effectively as a trustee. For information on legal issues, see *Charitable Status: A Practical Handbook* (details on page 131). However, it is important to start by answering two basic questions: 'What is a trustee?' and 'What are you letting yourself in for when you become a trustee?'

First, by becoming a trustee, you are joining the voluntary sector. There are currently around 170,000 general charities in the UK (*The UK Civil Society Almanac 2010*, NCVO), each with its own board of trustees, with a combined annual income of around £33 billion. Between them they have assets of over £90 billion and employ nearly 650,000 people. And who knows how many hours of voluntary work are clocked up by the millions of people who volunteer each year. The only thing we can say for sure is that they dwarf the hours given by paid staff.

They cover an enormous range of activities, from the arts to the environment, from health to welfare, from educating pre-school children to caring for older people in poor health, from maintaining the nation's heritage to providing accommodation for homeless people.

> *The most rewarding thing about being a trustee is seeing things happen in the community.*

Voluntary organisations are not the only ones working in these areas. Government and the private sector are also active here, providing services targeting individuals and their communities. Indeed there is increasing competition between the different sectors, with voluntary organisations often competing against private sector companies for government contracts. However, there are clear differences in how voluntary organisations do things compared with the public and private sectors. For example:

- Voluntary organisations do not make profits; any surpluses at the end of the year are ploughed back into the work of the charity rather than distributed to shareholders.
- Compared with the government and corporate sectors, this 'third sector' of voluntary and community organisations is tiny. The annual

turnover of Tesco is bigger than the entire voluntary sector; Cancer Research UK's income is about two per cent of that of Marks & Spencer; all the health charities combined could probably keep the National Health Service going for about a fortnight. In fact, most registered charities in England and Wales have an annual income of under £10,000.

- Voluntary organisations are not under the control of politicians or political appointees.
- Many voluntary organisations rely heavily on volunteers to do their work. It is estimated that over 20 million people a year will do some voluntary work for a charity or voluntary organisation.

This is by no means an exhaustive list. However, it does illustrate the point that voluntary organisations have a particular role to play in society. They cannot replace government; their motivations are different from those in the private sector; people view them differently from other sectors (how many people would willingly do unpaid work for their local bank or the local job centre?). And it is up to the trustees to define the particular role that their charity will play.

Trustees are also responsible, accountable and liable for the actions of their charity. One of the more sobering aspects of being a trustee is that you are a member of the group that will take the rap if anything goes seriously wrong. For example, if a charity does not have enough money to pay its bills this is deemed to be the responsibility of its trustees rather than its staff. Similarly, if a charity oversteps its constitutional boundaries (for example, if it provides services outside its permitted geographical area), such activities are illegal and the trustees will be held to account. The responsibilities and liabilities of trustees are a serious matter. The key ones are outlined later in this chapter, although you might also want to read up more fully on them elsewhere (the Charity Commission produces a range of useful publications – see page 127 for details).

So what, or who, is a trustee? Technically, charity trustees are the people who, according to the charity's constitution or governing document, are responsible for controlling the management and administration of the charity. Trustees may also be called management committee members, governors, council members or executive committee members. It doesn't matter what you are called; it is the function you have that determines whether or not you are a trustee.

We generally use the term 'management committee member' rather than 'trustee' in this book. This is because most voluntary organisations tend to refer to 'the management committee' rather than 'the trustees'. But even if the title varies, the role and legal status are the same.

Completing Checklist 1, *The legal and management framework* (page 98), will help you to think through the way that your management committee operates.

In practice, are you a full voting member of the management committee of your charity? And is your charity an independent body, with its own constitution? If so, you are a charity trustee.

### Key concept – governance

It is often said that the trustees' key function is one of **governance** rather than **management**.

**Governance** is the process a management committee uses to make sure that the organisation operates effectively, that it has a clear mission and strategy. However, governance is not necessarily about doing the work; rather, it is about making sure that things are done. For example, it is about ensuring that an organisation is well managed, but not necessarily about managing it. It is about making sure that the organisation has clear aims and priorities, policies and procedures, but not necessarily about forming them. It is about making certain that the organisation has appropriate systems, but not necessarily about developing them. It is about ensuring that the organisation has sufficient resources (people, equipment, expertise, etc.), although not necessarily about providing them. And so on.

(You may find it useful to turn to Checklist 2, *Governance*, page 100.)

**Management** is more about the day-to-day responsibilities of doing the work, delivering the services, appointing and supervising staff – in short, implementing trustee decisions.

So, for example, trustees should decide the amount of financial information they need to ensure that the organisation is progressing as planned; staff need to provide trustees with that information.

In practice, in smaller organisations, trustees may be involved both in the planning, decision-making and monitoring work (governance), and also in actually doing some or most of the work (management). Even so, it is worth being aware of the distinction between the two responsibilities so that if the organisation grows, the management committee can focus more on the governance side and staff on management. Also, it will help you to keep management committee meetings focused on the bigger picture of governance, instead of them getting too bogged down in the urgency and detail of management.

# What are the responsibilities of trustees?

## Taking personal responsibility

As a management committee member you accept personal responsibility for the activities of your organisation. This personal responsibility is shared between you and the other committee members. You are expected to know and understand your role. Ignorance is no excuse.

You are generally considered to have supported the decisions made by committee members unless you can demonstrate your active opposition to them. Disagreeing at meetings before a consensus is reached is not enough. If you disagree on a matter of importance, your active and continued opposition should be recorded in the minutes. Even then, if you continue to serve as a management committee member you are generally held to be jointly responsible, including for a decision that you voted against.

## Avoiding conflicts of interest

Charity trustees must act solely in the interests of their charity, irrespective of how they were appointed. For example, local councillors often sit on the management committees of local charities. However, they are not there to represent the local authority's interests and wishes; they, like their fellow trustees, should have the charity's best interests in mind. This applies equally to the management committee member who is also a beneficiary of the charity (and therefore stands personally to gain or lose from certain decisions) as to the trustee who is a friend or relative of someone tendering for a contract of work.

Management committee members should always try to avoid putting themselves in a position where their duty to act in the charity's best interests conflicts with their personal interests. If they cannot, they should declare this conflict of interest and usually withdraw from any further discussion on the matter. It's a good idea to have 'Declarations of interest' as a standard item on management committee agendas, just to enable trustees to declare any potential conflicts of interest that may arise during the meeting. This then allows the trustees as a group to decide whether these conflicts are serious enough for that trustee to leave the room while the item is being discussed.

## Acting with care

At all times, you are expected to act reasonably, in the interests of your beneficiaries and with a high standard of care. 'Reasonably' is usually taken to mean what an ordinary person in that situation would consider reasonable. If you are a charity trustee, failing to act reasonably and with care may put you in breach of trust. This may make you personally liable for any debts or claims which result from your actions.

It's worth bearing two concepts in mind here – duty of care and duty of prudence:

- **Duty of care** is about using reasonable care and skill in your work as a trustee, using your personal skills and experience to ensure that charity is well run and efficient. You should look at getting specialist, including professional, advice when needed. For example, you may think that the trustee board does not have sufficient knowledge to make an informed decision about an aspect of the charity's work or operations. Or there may be a particular and potentially serious risk to the charity. Or you may be concerned that you will in be in breach of your duties and powers as a trustee.

- **Duty of prudence** is more about acting honestly and reasonably to make sure that the charity is and will remain solvent and that you use charitable funds and assets reasonably and only in the furtherance of the charity's objects. This is not saying that you can never take risks, but rather that risks are calculated and reasonable and will not put the charity's assets or reputation at undue risk.

In layperson's terms these duties are simply trying to say that you should act carefully and, most importantly, know when you are or might be getting out of your depth. If in doubt take advice from someone who knows what they're talking about and is competent to give that kind of advice.

## Keeping an eye on finances

You need to be particularly careful about finances. You must be satisfied that the organisation is in control of its financial planning (budgets) and monitoring (regular reports on progress, sometimes called management accounts), that forecasts are reasonable and that progress is assessed regularly. You also need to guard against fraud, and ensure that safeguards are in place regarding matters such as handling cash and opening the post.

The general rule is that if you see problems looming, act sooner rather than later; don't just hope that things will turn out all right. As mentioned above, you can become personally liable for the debts of your charity.

## Obeying the law

You must make sure that legal requirements are met. The most important requirement is to make sure that the organisation works entirely towards fulfilling its objectives and works in accordance with its constitution. Any money given to you must be used for the declared charitable purposes of your organisation and also for any precise purposes for which it was given. Charity trustees could be asked to make good any money spent on projects which were outside the charitable purposes of their organisation.

Having said all of this, it is easy to be intimidated by your responsibilities and possible liabilities, to the point where you are put off completely. Try to keep a balanced view. Use your responsibilities and liabilities to remind you and your fellow trustees to act carefully ('prudently' in legal terms), lawfully and in accordance with your constitution – but don't let them bog you down completely. Be particularly careful when entering into major contracts or borrowing large sums. If you get this wrong and you end up owing more money than the charity has, you will be in a potentially difficult legal situation and will need to seek professional advice. There are ways of limiting your personal liability, such as insuring against fraud or setting up a registered company (charitable incorporated organisations may become another option; see *Charitable Incorporated Organisations* on page 131), although these are not always appropriate for a small organisation. See *Charitable Status* for more on this – details on page 131. But remember, your best defence and your best protection is to act sensibly and reasonably, with due care.

# Can trustees be paid for their trusteeship?

The answer is generally no, and certainly not unless you have express power (permission) from your constitution, the Charity Commission or the courts. Trusteeship is usually voluntary. You give your time willingly and not for personal gain. This is one reason why paid members of staff generally cannot (and should not) be trustees. They can attend trustee meetings if the committee so wishes; indeed that is often a good idea. It is normal practice for the chief executive (if there is one) to attend committee meetings, often accompanied by the finance manager. Other members of staff can also be invited to attend if there is an agenda item relating to their work. However, staff members can only speak and advise; they cannot and must not vote. This rule also applies to current beneficiaries of charities who receive benefits with a financial value from the charity.

You can claim for travel expenses and childcare costs incurred by attending trustee meetings and other trustee business; you can claim the cost of training courses and conferences connected with your trusteeship; you can even claim back the cost of buying this book. Basically, you can claim back any money that you pay out to fulfil your obligations as a trustee. However, it is difficult to claim compensation for lost earnings while attending to trustee business. You should certainly not be paid an honorarium or annual retainer, however small. You are giving your time, enthusiasm, skills and commitment to something that you think is worthwhile – and you are giving them for free.

The Charities Act 2006 did make it easier, however, to make some payments to trustees (or their businesses) for doing other work for the charity. The Charity Commission supports the principle of voluntary trusteeship but recognises that there are cases where it is in a charity's interests for a trustee to be paid or for a beneficiary to be a trustee. Tread pretty carefully in this area. For more information see *Trustee Expenses and Payments* (CC11) and if in doubt seek advice from the Charity Commission.

# 2 Who can be a trustee?

## Legal requirements

There are certain legal requirements governing who can be a trustee. You cannot be a trustee if you:

- are aged under 18 (unless the charity is a registered company, in which case the minimum age is now 16)
- have been convicted of an offence involving dishonesty or deception, unless the conviction is regarded as 'spent' (i.e. there has been a statutory period of rehabilitation, during which time you have committed no further offence)
- are an undischarged bankrupt
- have been previously removed from trusteeship of a charity by the court or the Charity Commission
- are under a disqualification order under the Company Directors Disqualification Act 1986.

It is an offence to act as a charity trustee while disqualified, unless the Charity Commission gives a waiver under section 72(4) of the Charities Act 1993. So if this applies to you, either don't stand for appointment as a trustee in the first place or, if you are already a trustee, resign.

## Practical requirements

It is equally important to look at the positive contribution you can make. You must be committed to the aims of the charity and able to give sufficient time to your role as trustee. This includes, as a minimum:

- attending trustee meetings and the annual general meeting
- reading papers before each meeting
- making a contribution during meetings
- making decisions in the best interests of the charity
- ensuring that the minutes of meetings accurately reflect discussions and decisions
- making sure that you know enough about the charity to make informed decisions on its behalf.

However, trusteeship is much more than simple attendance at meetings, and you don't stop being a trustee in between meetings. You have to ensure that paid staff and volunteers are properly managed and supported, and that the organisation is being efficiently run and is financially sound.

You may also be able to make a particular contribution to the charity.

- You may have certain key skills or knowledge (for instance, as an accountant or IT specialist) that is extremely valuable and could cost the charity a lot if it had to pay for it.

    *I started off years ago as treasurer of the toy library when my daughter was a toddler – I have a maths degree and no one else seemed to have much of a clue. And it's kind of gone on from there. My daughter's doing her A levels now, so I'm not doing the books for the After School Scheme any more, thank goodness, but I'm still treasurer of the allotment association and the local residents' association. I can't imagine not being involved in some sort of community group.*

- You may know some of the influential people in the area where the charity works; these contacts can be worth their weight in gold.
- You may have experience of doing the same kind of work as the charity (for example, if the charity is about adult education and you have been a teacher or volunteer tutor on an adult literacy scheme); if so, you can use these skills and experience on behalf of the charity.

    *It was because of my health research work that I was invited to become a trustee of a small healthcare charity. It isn't really all that time-consuming, and I feel that I'm doing something a bit more real, if you know what I mean.*

- You may be an enthusiastic fundraiser or event organiser, or good at involving and motivating volunteers.
- You may be a volunteer yourself, and so know what things are like at the 'coal face'.
- You may be someone who is or has been a beneficiary of the charity, and so can speak on behalf of other users and potential users of the charity's services – this is vital information for your fellow trustees.

    *The organisation is the best thing that ever happened to me. When I first came to see them, I was at the end of my tether, but they helped me to get back on my feet. I was pleased when they asked me if I'd like to be a volunteer – it meant that they believed I had something to contribute. I did that for six months and it seemed to go OK, but I was stunned when they said I should come along to a committee meeting to see if I'd like to join. They're all professional people and local councillors and so on. But they said that they'd really like to have someone who'd seen it from the other side, so to speak...*

This is by no means an exhaustive list. However, you and the charity will get much more out of your trusteeship if you feel that you can make a special contribution on top of your basic duties and responsibilities.

The best management committees have different people contributing different skills. In that sense it's an advantage if you don't have the same experience and contacts as your fellow trustees. A committee full of accountants should mean that you have excellent financial systems, but you may have only a very narrow perspective on the organisation's wider work. However, a committee with no legal or financial expertise may find itself fairly regularly grinding to a halt through lack of specialist information in key areas.

# 3 Why be a trustee?

There are many different reasons why people become trustees. First, charities need them. No trustees, no charity. Trustees move on, the charity's needs change, and even in an established charity it is good to have the new ideas, new energies, new perspectives that new trustees can bring.

You should also find it personally highly rewarding and stimulating. You are putting your skills and enthusiasms to good use in a new environment. You are doing this because you think the charity is doing something really worthwhile.

> *The most rewarding thing about being a trustee is watching young people develop, grow in confidence and fulfil their objectives.*

> *I got involved because I believe in promoting organic practices, and this seemed to be a good way to do it.*

Being a trustee also offers a terrific opportunity to help change things for the better. All charities are – or should be – looking to make a positive contribution to society, whether this means improving the environment, helping children find new ways of learning or expressing themselves, giving communities better facilities, changing people's attitudes to others or generally improving the quality of life of individuals and communities. It is hard work; there are failures as well as successes. But as a trustee you should be able to look back with pride on the changes you have helped bring about, on the people who have grasped new opportunities – and your particular role in making this happen.

# 4 Why refuse to be a trustee?

No one is, or should be, forcing you to become a trustee. Just because a charity needs a trustee and thinks you fit the bill doesn't mean you have to say yes. If you don't agree with, or can't become particularly excited about, what the charity is doing, don't become a trustee. A useful guiding principle is to ask yourself whether you would become a member of this charity, raise money for it or become a volunteer (time permitting). If the answer to these questions is no, then you probably shouldn't become a trustee either. There may be nothing wrong with the charity; lots of other people – including your friends – may be diehard supporters and great evangelists for it. But if you don't rate it – with or without good reason – don't become involved.

You may feel you have nothing particular to offer. If this is just lack of confidence on your part, that should not stop you becoming a trustee. However, if all you can genuinely see yourself doing is turning up to meetings, saying little or nothing at them, and then voting with the majority, you will not be doing yourself or the charity any favours by becoming a trustee.

You may not have the time. Charities are great at saying 'it's only three or four meetings a year – not much to it really' when actually, as this book shows, it's never that easy. Be realistic about the time that you have and the time commitment that the charity can reasonably expect. And it almost always takes more time than you or the charity think.

Equally, it may be the charity that doesn't really want you and your contribution. Some charities see trustees as a legal necessity and nothing more. Or the other trustees may think that they know best, that theirs is the only way, and expect you simply to fall into line. That's not the most attractive prospect in the world. You may still want to join precisely because you are committed to what the charity is or should be about and you think the trustees need a bit of a shake up. That's absolutely fair enough and can be crucial in the development – or even survival – of some charities. However if you feel you are not going to derive much satisfaction from your involvement in one charity then find another where you and your contribution will be valued.

# 5 How long should you remain a trustee?

This is a difficult question. First, it will take you time to get up to speed as a trustee. You need to come to grips with what the organisation is doing, how it does it, its financial arrangements and how its particular group of trustees functions. It is also important to have continuity of trusteeship. If trustees keep coming and going, it will be much harder to generate a sense of purpose and organisational cohesion. Both these points are arguments for committing to being a trustee for a minimum of three years, but more likely for more than five years.

However, there is also the opposite danger that the management committee never changes, or that it remains dominated by a few longstanding members. This can make generating or accepting new ideas much more difficult. New proposals may be met by remarks such as, 'For those of you who are new, we've never done it like that,' as if this were the clinching argument.

It is important to maintain a balance between experience and fresh ideas. Some charities set maximum terms of service. For example, the constitution may state that each trustee is elected for a period of three years, after which they must seek re-election. The charity may add a rule that no trustee can be re-elected more than twice (making a maximum of nine years) before having a break. There is nothing to stop such a person standing again after they have had a year or more out (although there is no guarantee of being re-elected).

There is no requirement to have a maximum 'length of service' rule of procedure. However, it is important to look at trusteeship from two angles:

- Do you still feel motivated and committed, or are you burned out and rather disenchanted? If the latter, is it time to take a break?
- Is the organisation becoming too complacent, too set in its ways? Or does it actually need stability and continuity? It may be that you need to persuade people to stay, or that you should bring in new blood.

People become and remain trustees for all kinds of motives. They think it will help their standing in the community or their job prospects; they hope to make some useful business contacts; or they see themselves as a knight in shining armour coming to rescue some poor charity from the clutches of inadequate trustees. But ultimately trusteeship is about making a positive and willing contribution to something that you think is worthwhile. And that doesn't mean to say that you have to do it for ever.

# PART **TWO**

# Key roles of trustees

# 6 The role of the management committee

The management committee (or trustee group) is the governing body of a voluntary organisation. It is where the decisions are made. It is the body that is held to account for all the activities of the organisation and is the group responsible for ensuring that the organisation operates properly and effectively.

The role of the management committee can be summarised under nine headings.

## Giving direction to the organisation

The management committee should ensure that the organisation has a clear sense of direction and purpose. If you don't know what you are doing, how can you function effectively? This vision must be shared by all the committee members, and communicated to the staff and others.

One way of communicating your vision is through a mission statement. This is a short, clear statement covering some or all of the following: why your organisation exists, what you do, how you do it, who you benefit and where you work. Don't forget that your organisation's object(s) or purpose(s) should be set out in your constitution or governing document, and the description in the mission statement must be consistent with this.

However, your vision is not much use unless you can put it into practice. This requires planning. Many organisations write up their ideas in a strategic plan to help review developments and monitor progress. This may be done by the chief executive/director, but should be discussed and agreed by the management committee.

For more detail on giving direction to the organisation see *Understanding your organisation*, page 29.

## Managing people

You are responsible for making the very best use of the people at your disposal. This includes both paid staff and volunteers. You need to ensure that the organisation:

- finds the people it needs to do the work (recruitment and selection)
- helps new people to settle in so that they understand the organisation, its values and what is expected of them (induction)
- allocates tasks for them to do
- supervises and appraises what they do
- supports and advises them where necessary
- seeks to develop staff, giving them new skills, experiences and opportunities, providing training where it is needed.

Many of these tasks may be delegated to a sub-committee or to staff. However, it remains the overall responsibility of the management committee to ensure that the people who carry out your work do so as effectively as possible.

For more detail on managing people see *Understanding your staff and volunteers*, page 41.

## Managing finances

Your financial responsibilities are absolutely key to your role as a trustee. The trustees together are responsible for the financial health and good financial management of the organisation; for the money that comes in and goes out of the organisation. This includes ensuring that:

- bills and salaries are paid on time
- money received is banked promptly
- you have procedures for handling cash and signing cheques
- any surplus money is invested appropriately to obtain a good return
- you have annual budgets to show what money you expect to spend and receive
- you monitor progress against these budgets and, where necessary, revise your plans in the light of developments
- your annual accounts are produced on time and to the correct format
- in general, you don't make financial commitments that you cannot meet.

Although the more detailed financial accounting and planning may be done by others (say the treasurer or finance officer), all trustees remain responsible for the financial performance of the organisation. Each trustee must develop a basic understanding of finance.

For more detail on managing finances see *Understanding your finances*, page 49, and *Dealing with numbers*, page 111.

## Managing resources

Not only are you expected to manage the human resources (staff and volunteers) and financial resources (money) at your disposal, you are also responsible for ensuring that the other necessary resources are in place and in good order. This includes ensuring that:

- your property is kept in good order and meets the charity's needs
- your equipment is well maintained, correctly used and properly insured
- there are sufficient funds for the organisation to carry out its activities or, if not, that you have a workable fundraising plan.

For more detail on managing resources see *Getting the resources*, page 57.

## Managing the charity's reputation

The charity's good name and reputation is central to its health and progress. Much of this is just about doing the basics right – making sure that you provide a good service to your users, making sure that you treat your volunteers and staff properly, making sure that you pay your bills on time and such like. Without the basics in place a charity's reputation will suffer and word of mouth is the most effective way of building, or destroying, a charity's reputation.

However, there are times when you will need to do additional things both to enhance and protect your good name. This can include:

- ensuring that communication within the organisation is good so that users, staff, volunteers, funders and key contacts are all kept informed of what the charity is doing and how it is progressing
- seeking publicity for positive things – your news, events and successes
- minimising the damage of negative publicity, whether inside or outside the organisation.

This doesn't mean that you have to turn yourselves into a PR machine but it does mean that you continually reflect on how the charity's reputation is growing (hopefully) or what you need to do to turn your reputation around. It may be worth having a review at the last management committee meeting of the year which just looks at what happened in terms of your reputation over the past 12 months: what helped and what hindered, what will happen next year, what may happen next year and the steps can you take now to improve your reputation over the next 12 months.

## Managing yourselves

The management committee is responsible for managing itself. This includes:

- holding regular and effective meetings, where you share information and make decisions
- members feeling committed to the organisation and working together for the good of the organisation as a whole – it is a team effort
- having a full complement of management committee members, each understanding their role and making a positive contribution
- having a good balance of different skills and experiences on the committee so that you can make effective decisions, having looked at the skills required from a number of perspectives
- ensuring that each committee member receives enough information to make good, informed decisions.

For more detail on managing yourselves see *Getting the work done*, pages 73 to 89.

## The legal role

The committee must ensure that the organisation obeys the law – and there are quite a few laws to obey. For example: charity law, company law (for charitable companies), employment law, health and safety law, child protection and safeguarding legislation, equal opportunities law, data protection rules, and regulations relating to premises, insurance and protecting the public. You will also need to keep track of legislation affecting the particular areas in which your organisation works.

This book is not principally about your legal responsibilities, although we touch on this in *What makes a good trustee?*, pages 1 to 20. There is a good deal of information available from other sources. The Charity Commission produces free publications on various aspects of charity life, all written from a legal standpoint (see page 127 for more details). It also sends out a free newsletter to all registered charities and has a telephone helpline.

There is also a companion to this book, entitled *Charitable Status*, which gives you a basic overview of the law and your responsibilities.

However, a word of reassurance. You don't have to be a legal expert to be a charity trustee, you simply need to act sensibly. But don't be afraid to ask questions. If you feel you are out of your depth on a particular issue, seek advice from your fellow trustees, outside experts or the Charity Commission. As we said earlier, if you act prudently and in the best interests of the charity, you are unlikely to run into serious difficulties.

# Accountability

A person or an organisation becomes accountable when powers or resources are delegated to them. They have to account for the way in which they use these powers or resources. Accountability is not a one-way process; it flows in different directions.

There are various people who will be accountable to you as they are carrying out tasks that you have delegated to them. These include:

- staff and volunteers
- sub-committees
- contractors (for example, builders and electricians upgrading your premises, outside trainers running training courses for your organisation, consultants helping you draw up a business plan).

As a committee member you are accountable to a number of people and organisations:

- donors and funders – you should be spending their money in line with undertakings you made to them
- regulators and rule-makers – those who check that the money is being spent properly and your activities are allowed
- beneficiaries or users of your services
- members of the organisation (if they are different from your beneficiaries)
- the wider community that benefits from your work.

Some forms of accountability (such as producing annual accounts) are compulsory; others are a matter of good practice.

For more detail on accountability see *Being accountable*, page 67.

## Maintaining independence

The independence of management committee members is absolutely crucial. No charity or trustee should be controlled or manipulated by others, or simply act as a representative of someone else's interests. Even where an outside body or person has the right to appoint or nominate a trustee, once the trustee is in place he or she must make decisions solely in the best interests of the charity, irrespective of the wishes of the nominating body.

Equally, the management committee should be careful to ensure that the organisation has a good spread of income and that it does not become overly dependent on any single funder. (For more on creating a fundraising strategy, see *Getting the resources*, page 57.) Your main responsibility is to your beneficiaries; always try to maintain the freedom to act in their best interests.

## And finally . . .

Keeping your eye on these various balls, and taking necessary action, is the essence of good governance and being a good trustee. Always be prepared to ask the awkward – or even obvious – question, and make sure you find the necessary information to do your trustee job properly. That's what the rest of this book is about.

# 7 Understanding your organisation

As a trustee you have to get to grips with a number of issues and make key decisions. If you have a good understanding of what your organisation is about, and where it fits into the wider picture, you will have a solid base to do this. There are various elements to consider.

## Need

Your organisation was set up to respond to a need: for example, to provide affordable housing in your area, or safe places for children to play or for abused women to live, or to encourage participation in music and the arts. It is very easy to become so preoccupied with the running of the charity that you lose sight of the reason why you are doing it.

> *We'd been running successful courses for women returners for years –
> CV writing, confidence building, that sort of thing. But it was only
> when we started really listening to the women who came to our job club
> that we realised how important it was to add basic computer skills to
> the range of courses on offer. So many women saw having to use a
> computer as the main stumbling block to getting a decent job and,
> whether they were right or not, it was affecting their confidence quite
> badly.*

A prime trustee responsibility is to maintain enough information about the needs you are aiming to meet and how these are changing. Be particularly careful to listen regularly to the views of your users, beneficiaries and members – they will be a valuable source of ideas, insights and information.

## Vision

The management committee should share a vision of what it would be like if your charity were to achieve everything you want to achieve. Although it may be a long way into the future before it can be realised, this vision should help to inspire and motivate the organisation.

One of the most important tasks of the management committee should be to translate its shared vision into a clear, understandable set of aims. These aims are what the charity intends to achieve in the long term. You need to make sure they are:

- in line with your charitable objects (you should find these in the charity's constitution or governing document)
- clear and understood
- shared by as many people as possible associated with the charity – the management committee, staff, volunteers, users, beneficiaries and supporters
- kept up to date.

The aims should answer the question: 'Why does our charity exist?' They provide you with coherence and identity, give a sense of purpose to everything that you do, and govern the tasks, priorities and targets that you set to achieve your vision. If you lose sight of your aims, your charity will sooner or later lose its way completely.

The vision doesn't have to be a dazzling slogan crafted by a PR expert. It should just say simply and compellingly what you are about. The Samaritans' vision statement is really simple:

*The Samaritans' vision is that fewer people die by suicide.*

## Mission statement

As mentioned, many organisations unpack their aims and vision in short, clear statements of what the charity aims to do and how it aims to do it. This gives people a short, easily understood guide to what your organisation is about and provides a unifying focus for everyone involved. Again, to use the Samaritans' example:

*We work to achieve this vision by making it our mission to alleviate emotional distress and reduce the incidence of suicide feelings and suicidal behaviour. We do this by:*
- *being available 24 hours a day to provide emotional support for people who are experiencing feelings of emotional distress or despair, including those which may lead to suicide*
- *reaching out to high risk groups and communities to reduce the risk of suicide*
- *working in partnership with other organisations, agencies and experts*
- *influencing public policy and raising awareness of the challenges of reducing suicide.*

Or Cancer Research UK:

> *Our vision of beating cancer is an enormous challenge. These four purpose statements set out how we address that challenge:*
>
> 1 *We carry out world-class research to improve our understanding of cancer and find out how to prevent, diagnose and treat different forms of cancer.*
>
> 2 *We ensure that our findings are used to improve the lives of cancer patients.*
>
> 3 *We help people to understand cancer, the progress we are making and the choices each person can make.*
>
> 4 *We work in partnership with others to achieve the greatest impact in the global fight against cancer.*

Some organisations reduce their mission statements still further to a strapline or slogan which they put on all publicity. For example:

'Furnishing homes, furnishing lives' (The Furniture Resource Centre)

'Information and training for the voluntary sector' (The Directory of Social Change)

'Raising money, changing lives' (Church Urban Fund)

'For ever, for everyone' (The National Trust)

'For wild land and wild places' (The John Muir Trust)

'Cruelty to children must stop. FULL STOP.' (NSPCC)

All these are very basic summaries of the aims and activities of wide-ranging and complex organisations, but they put the core message across quickly and easily.

Your mission statement (and strapline if you have one) should be simple and jargon-free. You are not looking for glitzy advertising slogans. Rather, you are trying to lodge the basic idea of what you're about in the minds of people connected with your charity.

If you are stuck on writing a mission statement, ask each member of the management committee to write down in not more than three sentences what they think the organisation is about and why. Gather these together and identify the common themes and ideas so that you can weave them into a single statement. Then give this to someone who does not know your organisation. Ask them if it gives them an idea of:

- why you exist
- what you do
- how you do it
- who you benefit
- where you work.

# Priorities

Your aims are likely to be fairly broad and long-term. You will not be able to achieve them right away; if you did try to do everything all at once you would most likely end up doing most things badly and achieve little or nothing. So you need to set priorities.

Your priorities will focus the organisation on its key areas of activity. Some priorities are ongoing (such as setting and monitoring budgets each year), but they are no less important because of that. However, there will be particular issues, needs or areas of activity that you want or have to address in the reasonably near future.

## Example

Hamletsville Village Hall is facing financial problems. The management committee realises that there are broadly two problems:

1   The retired members of the village community do not use the hall in the daytime, so it is often left empty once the parent and toddler group has finished at 11.30am.

2   Some of the longstanding evening activities are now poorly attended, so the groups struggle to raise enough membership subscriptions to pay an adequate hire fee for the hall.

Therefore, the management committee sets two financial priorities for the coming year:

1   To set up a new lunch club for older people (a recent community survey showed there was particular demand for this). This is initially planned to take place two days a week, but that could increase if the demand is there.

2   To disband (or at least move to a less prime time) the indoor bowls league and set up a computer club in its place. The parish council has been awarded some government money and has offered to help with most of the costs of the club for the first two years because it is concerned about growing unemployment in the village.

The village hall committee is also concerned that the Disability Discrimination Act will require it to become properly accessible. The chief issue is that the main entrance is not suitable for wheelchair users, so the committee decides that the main door needs widening and a permanent ramp to the door installing.

Also, the caretaker will be retiring in the summer. Who will replace him?

Some of the priorities here are long-term and wide-ranging (such as the overall financing of the village hall); others are one-off processes (such as appointing a new caretaker). Addressing all of them, however, should help you fulfil the village hall's longer-term aims.

# Tasks

It is important to think through your aims, mission statement and priorities, and to keep coming back to them. Unfortunately, none of this actually gets any work done! You need to put your ideas into practice and make sure that you are working towards fulfilling your priorities. This involves being clear about who is doing what and how.

So, in the example of the village hall, who will tell the remaining five members of the bowls club that they can no longer use the main hall on a Tuesday evening? Who is going to run the lunch club? How will you get people to and from the club? Who will sort out the health and safety issues? And who is responsible for raising the money for the adaptations to the building and overseeing the work?

The management committee can delegate each of these tasks. Again, this is an example of the governance/management split (see page 5). The management committee can set up sub-committees, or delegate the detail to staff and volunteers (see *Getting the work done*, pages 73 to 89 for more information). However, the management committee must know what is planned for the year and make sure that things happen.

# Targets

It is vital to focus on results. Your organisation will mainly be judged on what it achieves rather than on its intentions. You may set up a lunch club but only have eight members rather than the 40 you expected. In one sense you would have fulfilled one of your priorities but you would still feel as if you have failed.

And if tasks are to be completed well and on time, it is a good idea to set targets for each one. Ideally, each target will be SMART:

Specific

Measurable

Achievable

Related to a priority or longer-term aim

Timed (that is, with a deadline date for completion)

Your target for the lunch club might therefore be to have 20 people attending two days a week after six months – but only if your research shows that there are enough older people in the neighbourhood to make 20 a reasonable target.

Again, the management committee may delegate the responsibility for setting targets, but you will still want to monitor progress and, where necessary, make adjustments to timetables and target numbers.

By seeing that there are clear aims, priorities, tasks and associated targets, the management committee has a framework against which to measure the organisation's progress, an effective way of checking that you are keeping within your constitution and a ready source of information on which to base reports to funders and other outside bodies.

> The NEEDS you were set up to meet define your VISION as unpacked in your MISSION STATEMENT which is then broken down into current PRIORITIES and TASKS which are given TARGETS against which you can measure your SUCCESS

## Strategic plans

Mark Twain wrote: *'If you don't know where you are going you are sure to end up somewhere else.'* Planning is essential, and trustees play a key management role in the overall planning of their organisation's work. It is especially important to think ahead and plan for the long term, so that you know where you are going and what resources you will need to help you get there. This is called strategic planning, and organisations often write up their ideas in a strategic plan.

A strategic plan should be a short document to help you organise your work, highlighting priorities and potential problem areas. It builds on the kind of planning processes outlined above. Strategic plans usually:

- look to the future (one to five years ahead)
- focus on what the organisation will do and, in general terms, how it will do it
- think about where the organisation fits within the world around it
- take account of the resources needed and where these will come from.

Although the trustees have particular responsibility for strategic planning, you must try to make use of the expertise and experience of your staff, volunteers and users of your service when drawing up your plans. This can also help them feel more involved in, and committed to, the work of the organisation. In fact, especially in larger organisations, the strategic plan is often drafted by the chief executive and senior staff and presented to the trustees for discussion and approval, rather than the trustees having to do all the work themselves.

## Drawing up a strategic plan

There are many ways of drawing up strategic plans. Here is a five-stage process:

1 Review the main achievements and weaknesses of your organisation over the last year. Try to include the views of staff, volunteers and users of your services. Ask yourselves and them:

   – What went really well? What were the positive results from your work? What has changed for the better? Why were you able to achieve all this?

   – What couldn't you do? What didn't go as well as you wanted? Why was this?

   – What stage is your organisation at? Is it new, well-established, in decline, dying?

2 Write down what you want to achieve in the next year or so. This will include your aims and priorities, but probably not tasks and targets or the document will be too long. However, you should still focus on results.

3 List all the factors that might help you to do this (for example, grants and other funding, changes in the law, new partnerships, more staff and resources, premises and equipment, public awareness). Next, list the factors that might hinder your progress. Then look ahead and take into account any changes in the outside world that would have an effect on your organisation (for example, a change of law or discontinuation of major funding programmes).

4 Write down the key things you will need to do if you are to achieve what you want to do, and the main resources you will need. Be realistic. Do not make plans on the basis of resources that you are unlikely to obtain.

5 Identify how you will judge your performance. What are the absolutely vital things that need to happen (sometimes called your 'critical success criteria')? How will you know when you have achieved them?

You then bring all this together in a single document that describes what you aim to do, how you intend to do it and what you need to do it with.

But remember, you may have a beautifully drawn up strategic plan; however, if none of the work actually gets done the plan is pointless. In other words, beware of SPOTS (Strategic Plans On Top Shelves). Who is responsible for ensuring that the strategic plan is a live, working document, rather than one that just sits there gathering dust?

## Keeping track of success

Success is important in lots of ways. Not only does it build excitement and commitment within an organisation, it is also very important for planning and funding purposes. It is much easier to build on success than constantly to counteract failure; and funders like to support successful rather than crisis-ridden organisations.

Management committee members should be careful to note and celebrate success with staff and volunteers. It is important that they feel valued and appreciated; it also shows that you know what is going on and are involved in and committed to the organisation's work.

You should also be able to talk knowledgeably and enthusiastically to outsiders (especially funders) about your key successes. There is nothing like success to persuade funders that you are a good organisation which will make excellent use of their precious money. One of the main questions funders now ask themselves when considering an application for money is not, 'Is this a good idea?', but rather, 'If we give them the money, will the organisation be able to deliver results?' Showing that you have a good track record of achievements is one of the best ways of building outsiders' confidence in your organisation.

As a management committee, make a list of your organisation's five major successes of the last three to five years. What was so significant about them and what did they enable you to do next? Why do they show that you are a good organisation?

If you are a new organisation, make sure that you document successes as soon as you have them, and build up and communicate a sense of achievement.

## Keeping track of history

Management committee members also need to know the key points in the organisation's development. These can include:

- when the organisation was set up
- when you received your first significant grant

- when you employed your first member of staff or your fifth volunteer (or whatever was a critical number)
- when you were first able to open all day, or three days a week, or whatever
- when you had your hundredth user
- when you moved into your first (or current) premises
- when you elected your patron
- when you had your first celebrity visit.

This list is by no means exhaustive. The key thing is to decide what were the particular milestones for your organisation. These may include some, all or none of the items on the list above. As with your main successes, you are looking for a list of, say, between five and ten key developments which show how far you have come, and how good and reliable your organisation is.

# Keeping track of others

There may be plenty of organisations operating in your local community or your field of work. Or yours may be the only one. You need to know where you fit, why you are different or unique, who else is doing similar things, who you work with, who you don't want to work with and – in general – why you are the best at what you do. There are various reasons for doing this:

- To justify your existence – there are currently thousands of charities in the UK, with more registering each year; in an increasingly competitive fundraising environment you will need to explain why you are the best people to be doing what you do.
- To build on your strengths – you can't do everything, so do what you do best (which, hopefully, nobody else is doing, or at least not as well as you).
- To minimise the threat of being overtaken by someone else.
- To be aware of new opportunities which you could exploit to do new things or strengthen the organisation.
- To be aware of potential partnerships or joint working arrangements which may open new doors and give you greater credibility.

Some organisations set up smaller development committees to think about these issues and then report back to the management committee. Whichever way you do it, it pays to be well informed about your organisation, its strengths and weaknesses, its successes and its background. It all helps you make good planning and strategic decisions.

# Policies

Policies are the broad frameworks within which your charity operates. They define and describe how you do things. They can be a good way for the management committee to feel reassured that the organisation is operating properly.

For example, an organisation working with young people should have clear policies on vetting current and new leaders, the ratio of leaders to young people, minimum numbers of male and female leaders, what happens when allegations against leaders are made, and so on. Such policies provide stability, as everyone involved can refer back to them for guidance on how best to proceed.

Similarly, all voluntary organisations should have policies on their financial management (sometimes called financial procedures). See *Understanding your finances*, page 49 for more information on this.

The management committee plays a vital role in making sure that the organisation has relevant policies. There is a danger, however, that policies grind the whole organisation down; that you think you have to have a policy for everything before anyone can do anything. The basic aim of policies is to help ensure that routine tasks (such as record keeping) are carried out consistently and that there are minimum standards for the organisation.

You must also revise policies in the light of current needs, circumstances and legislation. Just because something was relevant three years ago does not mean to say that it is now.

Producing a policy is often a question of formalising what currently happens, or what appears to be common sense. There are a number of areas that you should think through, and for some you may choose to have a written policy, for example:

- statements of principles or values which underlie the work
- employing staff and volunteers
- safeguarding of children and vulnerable adults, plus the volunteers and staff who work with them
- equal opportunities
- ethical or moral principles – such as who (if anyone) you will not take money from, work with or generally be associated with
- managing your finances
- dealing with conflicts and crises.

# And finally...

By now you may be feeling that you will never have time to assimilate all the necessary information. But don't despair! As a trustee you cannot be expected to know everything; you are simply expected to know enough to take sensible decisions. The rest of this book looks at different ways of organising information so that you can find what you need and can operate really effectively.

# 8 Understanding your staff and volunteers

People are usually the most important asset in any voluntary organisation. They are also often the most undervalued (or at least they may feel that way). Relations with your staff and volunteers are governed by a mixture of legal requirement and good practice. However, you should see your staff as your greatest resource rather than a potential legal minefield. And, just like any other asset, they should be managed and developed for the benefit of the organisation.

> After you have read this chapter, it's a good idea to complete Checklist 4, *Employment and volunteers*, page 103.

## Paid staff

The management committee becomes an employer as soon as you hire paid staff. You need to take this role seriously because:

- you are responsible for seeing that staff work effectively towards achieving the objects of the organisation. If they don't, you are not managing the organisation's resources effectively
- staff rely on you for their livelihood
- your organisation (and possibly even you personally) may face serious penalties if you do not obey the laws covering employment.

There is no single, right way to manage staff. You should develop a system that suits your organisation and ensure that it is implemented either by your director and managers, if your organisation is large enough to have these, or by the management committee if you supervise your staff directly. There are three general areas of policy to consider: staff development, equal opportunities and pay policy.

### Staff development

You need to invest in your staff, to nurture them by providing opportunities for learning and development. This will encourage:

- personal and professional development
- improved performance
- people to work better together
- the organisation to change and adapt to different needs and circumstances.

Staff development is often tackled under the following headings:

- *Recruitment and selection* – making sure that you produce accurate and realistic job descriptions and person specifications and that you advertise vacancies in the right places so that you attract and choose staff with the right skills and qualities for the job.
- *Induction* – preparing staff properly for their work.
- *Supervision* – ensuring that all staff are adequately supervised and can learn from their work and what they do (see *Appraising staff performance*, page 43).
- *Training and development* – encouraging staff to go on training courses that will help them develop; some organisations set aside a certain amount of money each year for training and development.

## Equal opportunities

You need to ensure that staff are employed fairly and that nobody is unfairly discriminated against. This is a matter of law as well as good practice. You can do this by:

- advertising job vacancies openly and widely
- adopting selection procedures which are fair and focus on the job to be done rather than the people you know and like

> *When we looked carefully at the job description, we realised that it wasn't essential for the job holder to be able to lift and carry heavy boxes, since we already had three members of staff who'd been trained in manual handling. What was crucial was the ability to use a computer, so we revised the person specification to reflect this.*

- providing regular supervision and training opportunities to help develop appropriate new skills
- considering flexible working practices (part-time options, job-shares, flexitime)
- taking account of childcare needs
- making sure that your premises are accessible to people with disabilities
- monitoring the make-up of the staff – in terms of race, gender, ethnicity and disability, for example – and the opportunities that these staff are offered (for instance, who receives promotion and training).

## Pay policy

Your salary bill is often your biggest single item of expenditure. You need to know how decisions about pay are made and consider:

- what pay agreements already exist
- what you need to pay to attract good enough applicants
- what you can afford to pay
- what other people in the organisation are paid and how each job relates to the others
- what similar jobs in other organisations are paid.

## A staffing sub-committee?

Staffing matters can take up a lot of time. Some of the above, especially your approach to flexible working patterns, are a matter for discussion and debate rather than absolute requirements. And these debates can become quite heated. Some organisations therefore set up a staffing sub-committee made up of people who have relevant skills and experience. The committee is usually charged with:

- developing and reviewing employment policies
- promoting and encouraging training and development opportunities
- advising on problems and issues as they arise
- keeping up to date with changes in employment law.

Whatever the particular role of the sub-committee, it must report back regularly and clearly to the management committee, which remains responsible for all staff and the decisions affecting them.

## Appraising staff performance

Trustees should ensure that a system of appraisals of staff performance is in place. It is usual to have a formal appraisal once a year, which is carried out by the employee's manager (and in the case of the most senior staff member, the organisation's chair, with regular (say quarterly) reviews of progress. The starting point for any appraisal should be the employee's job description, together with a set of targets that should have been drawn up and agreed at the beginning of the year. The appraisal can then consist of a discussion of:

- which targets were achieved over the last year, and how?
- which targets were not achieved over the last year, and why?
- what the employee and manager agree are the targets for the coming year

- what help the employee will need to meet these targets (such as training)
- how success will be measured.

The quarterly reviews assess progress towards achieving targets, revising them in the light of any changed circumstances and checking that enough support is being given.

Appraisals work best when:

- there is an atmosphere of trust and honesty
- the person being supervised is involved in assessing his or her own performance
- the process is linked to training and development rather than pay.

Some organisations operate a '360 degree' appraisal system where information is obtained from a range of colleagues who work with each employee. This can be a valuable opportunity for staff members to understand how they work with, and are viewed by, people at different levels within the organisation.

## The chief executive

Your senior staff member (chief executive, director, chief officer, or whatever they are called) is the key link between the staff and trustees. The relationship is potentially problematic because he or she:

- may have more relevant professional expertise than some of the trustees
- will often know more about the work of the organisation and yet is your employee.

To avoid problems:

- always bear in mind the distinction between governance and management (see page 5); respect the judgement of your senior staff member and give him or her the backing necessary to manage the organisation, but don't accept everything he or she says without question. Trustees need to get the right balance between support and challenge (or holding to account)
- keep the lines of communication open, so that you know enough about what is going on in the organisation to do your job as a trustee, without becoming bogged down in the detail.

It is difficult to supervise by committee, so the task of supervising the chief executive is often delegated to the chair of the trustees, who may need help and guidance in this role, for example from an outside mentor. It is usually a good idea to establish a framework of regular meetings where the chair and senior staff member can update each other and discuss current issues. These meetings can be an opportunity both to monitor and to offer support.

## Legal responsibilities

There is a massive amount of legislation affecting employees, their rights and responsibilities. There are separate acts on health and safety at work, sex, race and disability discrimination, equal pay and employment protection (and that is by no means all).

As an employer, you should issue all staff with a formal contract of employment. This will be similar to any contract that you have had yourself as an employee, setting out the responsibilities of the employer and the rights and responsibilities of each employee. There is a model contract of employment in *The Russell-Cooke Voluntary Sector Legal Handbook* published by the Directory of Social Change (the book's details are on page 131 – or your local council for voluntary service (CVS) may have a copy: see *Useful addresses*, page 121). Or you could base your contract on one produced by an organisation similar to your own. If you have a staffing sub-committee, its members could draft a contract of employment, which the management committee could then discuss and approve.

It is also essential to have a written procedure for discipline, dismissal and grievances, which does not form part of the contract but which is made available to all staff. Although you always hope you will never have to refer to it, it is much easier to be prepared in advance with policies and procedures, rather than to be faced with having to draft something under pressure when things start to go wrong, which will probably be too late (go to www.acas.org.uk/index.aspx?articleid=2175 to read the Acas Code of Practice 1 – Disciplinary and Grievance Procedures).

The management committee is also responsible for ensuring that income tax and national insurance are paid, on time, to Her Majesty's Revenue and Customs (HMRC). There are severe penalties if you fail to do this. If you are not sure exactly what to do, seek professional advice from your accountant or HMRC.

You need to have employer's liability insurance. Again, you will probably need to seek professional advice on the sort of cover that is available.

## Communicating with staff

Much of this book deals with the kind of information that you as a management committee member should be receiving. However, information must flow both ways. You need to make sure that your decisions and the reasons behind them are communicated effectively to everyone in the organisation. Otherwise, you will become remote from the day-to-day work and find it harder to make informed decisions.

It is also important to encourage staff and volunteers. Always try to:

- give positive feedback – it's easy to assume that people know when they are doing a good job and say nothing. Everyone needs encouragement
- give constructive criticism – people can only improve their work if they know which specific elements need to be improved. But try to be supportive rather than destructive.

# Volunteers

Volunteers are the life-blood of many voluntary organisations. In fact, the majority of charities in Britain have no paid staff at all, and even some of the very largest are heavily dependent on volunteers to deliver their services.

However, you need to think carefully about your approach to volunteers. Just because they give their time for free doesn't mean that you should accept any and everybody who walks through your door.

Volunteering is a two-way process. Volunteers give their time, energy and skills; in return they receive various non-cash rewards (such as personal satisfaction, skills development, the opportunity to make a difference). You need to make sure that volunteers have clear roles and are properly briefed and well looked after. They must also have the necessary skills to do a good job, be supervised effectively and generally bring credit to the organisation. To help you achieve this, you can use job descriptions and person specifications to recruit and manage volunteers as well as paid staff.

> *It was so encouraging to see people make the transition from using our services to volunteering to support other parents in similar circumstances. Some of our best mentors have been drawn from among our beneficiaries.*

It is good practice to develop a policy document or code of practice on volunteering. Volunteers are a vital and valuable resource for your organisation. They give you their time and energy to help you advance your aims, so it is only fair that you manage them properly and provide them with a rewarding and worthwhile experience.

*Now that I've retired, I've got too much time on my hands – and I do enjoy meeting people. I really look forward to my Monday morning stint at the job club. My role is just to welcome people and make them feel at home while they're waiting to see an adviser. Everyone says how much better the atmosphere is since we started this system. I feel that I'm part of a team that's doing something useful – and since I've got my bus pass, I don't cost them much!*

## Investing in your volunteers

Many of the issues covered in the section on paid staff above also apply to volunteers. You need to make sure that sufficient resources are allocated in the budget to recruit, select, train, supervise and organise your volunteers. Someone within the organisation should be responsible for ensuring that every volunteer is supervised and contacted regularly, that they have the chance to discuss and plan their work, and that they receive positive feedback. No volunteer should feel out of pocket as a result of their activities; each one should feel that the organisation really does believe in his or her unique contribution, recognise it and want it to grow and develop.

## Keeping volunteers motivated

Try to make sure that your volunteers:

- feel appreciated
- have a sense of belonging to the organisation
- feel part of a team with their co-workers
- are treated as working partners by paid staff
- receive recognition for their work
- are involved in some of the decisions which affect their work (such as setting objectives and solving problems)
- feel able to handle the tasks offered to them
- are given a chance for advancement and personal growth
- can see that their work makes a real difference.

## Volunteers and the law

There is a lot of legislation affecting volunteers. If they are receiving welfare benefits there are limits on what they can do and what they can receive in expenses. Equal opportunities legislation also covers volunteers, as do health and safety laws. If volunteers work with children you should have a child protection policy which takes into account important legal issues such as the need to get a Disclosure from the Criminal Records Bureau. Once again, many organisations have found it helpful to set up a sub-committee to oversee their policies and practices regarding volunteers or to include volunteers within the staffing sub-committee's responsibilities. The National Centre for Volunteering has helpful information on all aspects of volunteering (see *Useful addresses*, page 121, for details).

> After reading this chapter, turn to Checklist 4, *Employment and volunteers*, page 103 to find out if your organisation is making the most appropriate use of volunteers.

# And finally ...

In general, try to make a point of talking to staff and volunteers both to find out what they think and to prevent a 'them and us' attitude from setting in. Although there is almost always some distance between staff and trustees (and probably rightly so) you are all part of one organisation, dependent on each other to get things done. Each person has his or her own particular role, but the better the relationship between you all, the more effective everyone will be.

# 9 Understanding your finances

Trustees are not expected to be accountants; nor do they have to understand every last detail of the accounting process. However, they are responsible for the financial health and good financial management of the organisation, so it is vital that each trustee has a basic understanding of finance. *Dealing with numbers*, page 111, takes you through a set of figures.

Anyone who has managed their own household affairs will have a basic grasp of budgeting, record keeping and forward planning. You may also have had responsibility for financial management in the course of your own paid employment. It is likely that your organisation will have either a paid member of staff (book-keeper or finance officer/manager) or a volunteer treasurer, whose job this is. As an ordinary trustee your role is to make sure that:

- your organisation has a proper system of accounting
- you receive sufficient and regular information to oversee the organisation's finances effectively
- you understand the accounts and can interpret the financial information you receive
- the person who inspects or audits your accounts is happy with the way in which records are kept and accounts are produced, and has given your latest accounts a clean bill of health.

## Accounting systems

Your basic accounting system should tell you how you are doing financially. This includes:

- where your money comes from (income accounts)
- what you spend money on (expenditure accounts)
- whether your income is greater or less than your expenditure (surplus or deficit)
- what income and expenditure are planned for the future (budgets)
- what are your assets and liabilities (balance sheet) – assets are positive items such as cash in the bank, investments and money owed to you; liabilities are negative items such as money that you owe

- what return you are receiving from investments and money in bank accounts (investment policy; use of cash balances). If you are joining an existing organisation (rather than setting one up from scratch), make sure you understand how the current accounting system works.

> Completing Checklist 5, *Finances*, page 106 will help you to judge if your organisation's procedures are appropriate.

## Information from the accounting system

Your accounting system is the basis for the financial information that the organisation needs for its own internal purposes (your management accounts – see *Budgeting and financial planning*, page 52) and for external reporting (annual accounts).

Larger organisations will do their accounts on computer; smaller organisations may keep handwritten records. Whichever system you use, you need to make sure that it is accurate and backed up by evidence (invoices, receipts, lists of cheques paid in and so on).

Charities have to keep their accounts in a certain form. Most are governed by the Statement of Recommended Practice, known as the SORP, issued by the Charity Commission. The precise form of your annual accounts depends on your income.

Here is a very rough guide as to what to expect:
- Charities which are not companies and whose income is £250,000 or less can prepare basic receipts and payments accounts. They can have them independently examined (unless their constitution says they have to be audited).
- Charities which are not companies with a gross income of £250,000–£500,000 in the relevant year must prepare their accounts on an accruals basis in line with the SORP (including a balance sheet, statement of financial activities and explanatory notes). They can have them independently examined (unless their constitution says they have to be audited). There are rules as to who can do this independent examination if the charity's income is over £250,000.
- Charities which are not companies and have a gross income of over £500,000 in the relevant year must prepare their accounts on an accruals basis (see above). These accounts must be audited by a registered auditor.

- Charitable companies must prepare their accounts on an accruals basis and produce a directors' report which conforms to both company and charity law (the SORP gives guidance on this). The audit requirements vary slightly according to the size of the charity.

These are minimum requirements. Charities can elect to have audited accounts even if their income is below £500,000, or prepare full accrual accounts if their income is under £100,000.

Please note that the situation can change fairly regularly. The Charity Commission website is excellent for giving details on which kinds of accounts you need to prepare and who needs to inspect them.

Unless you are the treasurer, you are not expected to know the details of all the above. *The Charity Treasurer's Handbook* provides more information for those who need it (see page 130 for details). However, you must read and understand your annual accounts and seek clarification where necessary. It is always useful to compare this year's accounts with last year's to see what has changed, and find out why.

You also need to look at whether you are making a surplus (profit) or a deficit (loss). You may have made a deficit for perfectly understandable short-term reasons. For example, last year you might have decided to spend some of your reserves on buying three computers and a photocopier. Although you are confident that they will more than pay for themselves in future savings, this may have meant that you made a loss for the financial year in question. Alternatively, your deficit may indicate more fundamental financial problems that require some hard thinking. Large deficits also present fundraising problems, because funders will be concerned that you are financially incompetent or are gradually (or not so gradually) going bust. You may therefore want to attach a note to your accounts clearly explaining the situation, why it arose and what you are doing about it.

Surpluses are generally good news – unless they are too large, in which case they can present fundraising problems as well, because it could appear as if you can't use all your financial resources. Again, you might want to explain in your accounts if, for example, you received a large grant at the end of the financial year which will be spent over the following year, or if you are retaining reserves in line with prudent financial planning (see page 52).

# Budgeting and financial planning

Your annual budget is your financial plan for the year ahead and a key management tool. It helps you to control expenditure and gives you advance notice of the income you need to raise. Make sure that the budgeting process is started early enough (at least six months before the start of the next financial year) to give you time to make critical decisions about staff recruitment or the level of your charges to users, for example. Although it is usually left to the treasurer (or paid staff) to draw up the budget, all trustees must be involved in the process. You need to:

- check that the budget reflects the organisation's plans and priorities. Are you focusing resources on the work that is most important?
- check the reasoning behind the figures. Will income actually rise as predicted? Why are costs increasing in any particular area?

The budget is then broken down into monthly or quarterly estimates of income and expenditure, because not all money comes in or goes out evenly over the year. You might have weekly income and expenditure from your lunch club, but the income from your annual garden party might all come in during July while the expenditure is mainly incurred in August, with a deposit cheque for the venue and marquees due the previous November. Try to predict under each budget heading in which month money will come in and go out. You will then have a useful monitoring tool (see *Management accounts*, page 54).

There is a tendency within the budgeting process to overestimate income and underestimate costs to make things look good. In practice, income tends to be lower than anticipated and costs higher. Make sure that you stress these points in your discussions, until you are satisfied that your budget is a reasonable and realistic document. The current year's figures will often be a guide to what you can expect, unless you are predicting a significant change in your activities.

You also need to budget for reserves.

## Reserves

Although as charity trustees you are under a legal obligation to use charity funds within a reasonable time of receiving them, you also need to plan carefully for the future. You need to have funds to protect the organisation in case you run into cash flow problems, or a regular grant is suddenly cut, or you experience a general downturn in income. Alternatively, there may be a new piece of legislation that means you have an unexpected jump in costs (to conform to new health and safety regulations, for instance), or your rent may be doubled after a rent review, or you may need to make some staff redundant.

More positively, it is always useful to have money that you can spend on the development of the organisation. For example, you may decide to buy in outside help to look at some key policy areas, to invest in IT, to produce new information booklets or to undertake a major marketing and publicity operation.

All of this means that each charity should aim for a level of reserves which helps it to guard against problems and make the most of opportunities. Reserves are simply extra money in the bank (or invested elsewhere) that you can spend on any part of the charity's work or development. A reasonable level of reserves is now seen as a sign of good management, of taking sensible precautions in an increasingly volatile charity world.

Most organisations now aim to have at least the equivalent of three months' income as reserves. So, for example, if your annual income is £60,000, you would have at least £15,000 in the bank at the end of the year, after all bills are paid. Some organisations aim for a much higher level – as much as one year's income. You need to decide what level of reserves is appropriate to your organisation, plan how you aim to reach your desired level and budget accordingly. You may need to do this over a number of years.

## Cash flow

Cash flow refers to the flow of money in to and out of the organisation, and when you expect these transfers to happen. If your experience up to now has been as an employee of a large company, you may never have had to worry about cash flow. In a small charity where you have limited cash in the bank, cash flow can become a real issue. For example, although you may be budgeting for a surplus on the year as a whole, your main grant may not come in until after you have had to pay some big bills. So will you have enough money to cover these bills? Or what if a grant is paid later than you were anticipating? Will this mean your account goes overdrawn?

*I was so embarrassed. I'd completely forgotten that we'd have to pay everyone's travel expenses on the spot, even though we weren't paying for room hire or the tutor till the end of the month. We had to find over £100 in petty cash just when our bank balance was at rock bottom!*

Your cash flow forecast is a monthly estimate of when money is due to come in, when it will be paid out and how much will be left in the bank. It should enable you to track progress and ensure that you can pay salaries, bills and expenses on time. If the organisation's account is expected to go overdrawn, you can then make arrangements in advance.

## Management accounts

Management accounts compare the organisation's actual income and expenditure with the budgeted figures. Sadly, writing things down in a budget, however carefully, does not guarantee that they will turn out as planned. Management accounts are usually produced monthly in larger organisations and quarterly in smaller ones. Each income and expenditure budget heading is compared with the actual figure (taken from your accounting system) for the year up to that point. Trustees should then:

- note any significant differences between the budget and actual figures (for income and expenditure)
- try to understand why these have occurred
- discuss whether you need to take any action – the discrepancy may be a one-off blip or it may be part of a longer-term trend
- discuss whether you need to revise the budget in the light of this.

You need to strike a balance between not panicking at the first sign of trouble and not leaving things too late in the hope that problems will solve themselves. In general, try to keep a lid on costs. It is much easier to control expenditure than it is to raise extra income. Discussing your financial position should be an agenda item at every trustees' meeting.

*Dealing with numbers*, page 111, gives much more detail on reading management accounts.

## Basic procedures

It is also worth checking that the basic accounting procedures are being followed through. For example, it is vital that:

- all money and assets are used solely to pursue the objects of the organisation as set out in its constitution
- full, accurate accounting records are kept securely for at least seven years
- bank accounts are operated properly and cheques are signed by more than one person

- cheques are not signed without details of the amount of the payment and the purpose for which it will be spent
- all payments are backed up by a source document (such as an invoice or a bill – larger organisations may also use purchase orders)
- petty cash payments are backed up with receipts
- all grant money is spent in accordance with the terms on which it was awarded
- the monthly payroll is checked and authorised by a senior staff member or trustee (and certainly not left to just one person to do)
- all necessary tax and national insurance is deducted before making payments to staff or for casual labour.

This may all be familiar to you from other contexts, but you may not be aware that if you are a registered charity with an income over £10,000 you must also include the words 'registered charity' (and preferably your charity number) on headed notepaper, cheques, invoices, orders, publications, publicity material and other official documents.

## Finance sub-committee

Finance is one of those areas particularly suited to a sub-committee. The finance sub-committee is charged with regular scrutiny of the management accounts and any issues arising from them. The treasurer (or chair of the sub-committee if you don't have a treasurer) then reports to the full trustees' meeting. However, remember that even when the detailed scrutiny of figures is delegated, you and all the other trustees remain legally responsible for your organisation's finances.

## And finally . . .

In general, if you feel uncomfortable around figures or you cannot understand the information you receive, ask for help from your fellow trustees or a suitable person outside the organisation. Don't be embarrassed; it may simply be that the information is being produced badly or is unnecessarily complicated. There is plenty of training around to help you understand accounts. Whatever you do, don't assume that you can simply leave it all to the others; they may be just as bewildered as you are.

# 10 Getting the resources

The management committee is responsible for making sure that the organisation has enough money to stay solvent, and to maintain and develop its work for the benefit of its current and future users. This usually requires some fundraising, whether this involves a series of coffee mornings or major applications to grant-making trusts. Once again, the trustees remain responsible for all the fundraising activities of the charity, although they may do very little fundraising themselves.

Trustees are under an obligation to preserve and make best use of the assets and resources at their disposal, including ensuring that money is not left lying around in non-interest-bearing bank accounts.

This chapter starts with fundraising and then moves on to managing your assets.

## Fundraising

Your fundraising activities and tactics can say a lot about your organisation. It is usually through your fundraising that most people come into contact with you, so you need to get it right. Your donors will be concerned both about how you raise your money in general and what you will do with their donation in particular. So, as a trustee you need to ensure that:

- fundraising is undertaken properly
- the purpose of any appeal is clear and accurate
- you do not use methods which exert undue pressure on people to give or which your supporters may find distasteful for other reasons
- you obey the law
- money raised is properly accounted for.

You should be clear from the outset about how much you need to raise, your strategy for doing this, and where the organisation will find the necessary resources (time, expertise, people, materials, administration) to achieve success. You can then monitor progress towards your target at regular intervals and keep a watchful eye on your fundraising costs.

## Ethics

You should also have a policy on whom you will and will not take money from. For example, the Big Lottery Fund derives its money from gambling. Or perhaps a local company that has just offered you a £5,000 grant for your children's play area has suddenly laid off 300 people. Does this matter? Does it matter where your funders invest their money? And would you accept money from your local authority if in return it required a place on your management committee or a right to see your management committee papers and minutes?

These are the main rules on such ethical decisions:

* It is not what you as an individual trustee thinks that counts. Your personal likes and dislikes are irrelevant. It's the best interests of the charity that matter. For example, you may be a trustee of an environmental organisation and you don't approve of nuclear energy. This doesn't necessarily mean that the charity shouldn't apply to British Nuclear Fuels Limited, say, for money. However, if the trustees know that taking money from the company would risk alienating your supporters then it would be perfectly reasonable not to apply. The National Childbirth Trust (NCT), which among other things promotes breast-feeding, once caused a bit of a storm among its members over whether it should accept money from Sainsbury's. The objection was that Sainsbury's markets its own brand of formula milk and that this goes against what the NCT believes.
* If you want to reject a gift (certainly a major gift) on ethical grounds, you should first contact the Charity Commission for its advice or approval.

Basically, there is no right or wrong on ethics other than what is appropriate for your charity, its members and its users. However, it is better to decide beforehand what you will and won't do and plan accordingly.

## Six key fundraising concepts

1 Fundraising is about personal relationships. Somebody asks somebody for money. The better these two people know, like and trust each other, the more likely the potential donor will be to give. A lot of fundraising, especially at the local level, boils down to whom you know. If you don't know enough of the right kind of people yourselves, you might want to recruit into the organisation people

who do, and get them to use these contacts to raise money (see *Organising your fundraising*, page 62).

2   Fundraising is about change, rather than money. Donors give to help improve people's quality of life, or to protect the environment, or to support the arts, or whatever. Therefore, your fundraising approach should be to explain how you change things for the better rather than simply stating what work you do.

3   Fundraising tends to be about individual pieces of work (sometimes called projects) rather than the organisation as a whole. For example, an overseas aid charity will place an advert featuring a starving child in a newspaper and say, effectively, 'Help us work with people like this.' This is a much more powerful fundraising proposition than simply saying, 'Please give whatever you can to Save the Children.' Or a hospital will have an appeal for a new scanner rather than ask for a general contribution to hospital funds. Similarly, you may need to break up your organisation's work into individual chunks and raise money for each one.

### Examples of projects

- An alcohol recovery organisation raising money for an alcohol awareness programme in schools
- A community centre raising money for a new roof or a disabled toilet
- An arts organisation raising money for an exhibition of paintings by local children
- A conservation organisation appealing to save an area of outstanding natural beauty or a fine building
- A mental health organisation raising money for an awareness programme to combat prejudice about mental health

4   Fundraising must be relevant. Just because people or institutions have money doesn't mean that they will be interested in you. Make sure that you or your fundraisers have a good reason for contacting each person you write to or ask for a donation. If there isn't one, don't bother; concentrate your energies on more fruitful sources instead.

5   Most of your money may come from a few key supporters or a few key activities (such as a regular fundraising event). It's very easy to take these for granted and put all your fundraising energies into pursuing new sources of income. This is a recipe for disaster. People who have given before are the most likely to give again, as long as you have looked after them. The book *Looking after your Donors* covers this in detail (see page 129 for information).

6    You can't tell funders everything – there isn't time and they won't listen to (or read) it all. So tell them about what is most likely to interest them.

## Sources of income

The general public are still by far the biggest givers to charity (currently giving about £10 billion a year, £2 billion of which is left in wills). They give through collections, fundraising events, sponsored events, radio and television appeals, direct mail requests, lotteries, because they are members of the charity or simply because a friend asked them. There is no limit to the ways in which you can persuade people to give, and some of the oldest forms of fundraising (especially sponsored events) remain some of the best. There are plenty of books available which will tell you more.

Grant-making trusts are charitable bodies that exist to donate money to other charities. Each has its own interests, priorities and procedures. There may be local trusts in your area and there are also trusts that give throughout the UK (including well-known foundations such as the BBC Children in Need Appeal). Collectively they give over £3 billion a year. There are directories that list trusts and what they will fund (see *Publications*, page 127). You may need to decide whether to invest in copies of these or to consult them through your local council for voluntary service (see page 123) or public library.

The National Lottery was set up to generate funds for charity. It currently channels over £1 billion a year to charities, the arts, sports and heritage projects, plus the London Olympics. There are different distribution boards, each with its own interests and, unfortunately, fairly complex applications procedure. The main one for charities is the Big Lottery Fund, which distributes over £600 million a year. However, there is also an excellent small grants scheme (Awards for All) for grants under £10,000. See page 125 for contact details.

Companies give around £300 million a year in cash to charities, plus a lot more in other forms of giving. Most receive far more appeals than they can handle, but many are from people or organisations they don't know. One of the best ways of raising money from a company is through their employees (for instance, persuading an employee who knows you and your work to raise money for you and to ask their company to match their fundraising), or through personal contacts with the company chair or managing director. Again, directories are available which give contact details for companies that make donations.

Government gives around £11 billion a year to charities, mainly in the form of contracts for agreed work. Much of this comes through local authorities and health authorities and often consists of payments for basic services (such as meals on wheels or childcare and health advice work). There are also major government funding programmes. The best way to find out about these is via www.governmentfunding.org.uk (see page 128).

More and more charities are now earning income from selling goods and services. Some charge for the services they offer; some sell goods made by the charity's beneficiaries; some sell t-shirts, Christmas cards and donated goods. You should note that trading through shops or catalogues usually doesn't make anything like the profits people assume, so enter into such activity carefully.

## Planning your fundraising

Fundraising, like anything else, needs planning. Your organisation's strategic plan will highlight the main developments that are anticipated over the next one to three years. Each development can be costed and fundraising targets set. Your annual budget shows what income is needed to keep your current activities going over the next year.

In addition to costing your work, you will need to consider your fundraising costs. The biggest item of expenditure is likely to be the salary of a paid fundraiser or fundraisers – if your organisation has reached this stage in its development. Even if it hasn't, you will still be faced with decisions: should you subscribe to the online funding databases? Do you need donor management software? What about your public image? Is this the year to spend money on a logo and professionally designed leaflets? If all of this is going to be too expensive, are there other ways of obtaining the resources that you need? What does your local CVS have to offer? Can you obtain sponsorship from a local company?

Much of your fundraising may be regular and ongoing. The further you move away from this core support, the more expensive and time-consuming it becomes. So, try to think strategically about your current fundraising:

- Who are your current supporters?
- Why do they support you? What are their interests and concerns? Is any of this likely to change?

- How can you strengthen your relationship with your existing supporters?

It may be that by simply retaining the loyalty and commitment of your current supporters you can continue to raise all the money you need.

The next stage is to look at potential new supporters (see *Sources of income*, page 60):

- Which people or funding bodies do you plan to attract as supporters in future?
- What are their interests and concerns? And, crucially, why should they be interested in your work?
- Realistically, what are your chances of raising money from them?

All donors have particular interests and concerns; the fundraising challenge is to show that you address these concerns.

## Organising your fundraising

The management committee should think through who will do the work of asking for money. This will depend on who is willing, who has the skills and time and whether you have or can take on staff to do it.

If you employ fundraising staff you can expect them to do most of the fundraising leg-work. However, trustees often still play a very active part here, particularly in making direct approaches to individuals, trusts and companies and, in general, making maximum use of their personal contacts.

You may decide to delegate the fundraising to a committee. The members of a fundraising committee do not all have to be trustees, although, like any other committee, it should report back to the trustees regularly. The committee's main responsibilities are drawing up the fundraising plan and making sure it is put into practice. This may involve:

- delegating some of the fundraising tasks (such as writing grant applications) to existing staff
- bringing people with good contacts on to the committee – they can help ask for money
- employing and managing a fundraiser (subject to budgetary approval by the trustees)
- setting up other sub-committees to undertake particular aspects of fundraising (such as organising events or obtaining legacies)

- setting up an appeals committee to organise and oversee a large fundraising appeal.

The fundraising committee should be made up of people who are committed to raising the money, who enjoy doing it and have the appropriate skills. But overall responsibility for ensuring its success still lies with the management committee.

---

### Getting the max

There are various tax incentives to encourage people to give which you should try to take advantage of. The main one is Gift Aid, which is worth around £1 billion a year to charities. Charities can reclaim the tax on any donation made by any taxpayer as long as:

- the donor provides a Gift Aid declaration, and
- the charity maintains an 'audit trail' linking the payment to the donor – in other words, as long as the charity records each donation separately so that it can prove to HMRC how much each donor has given.

The Gift Aid declaration can state that it covers all donations from the date of the current gift onwards, so one declaration covers all future claims. There is, however, a limit on the level of benefits the donor can receive (broadly, 2.5% of the value of total donations, up to a limit of £250).

So, in theory, you can add 28% (on current tax rates) to the income from a sponsored run if:

- all your sponsors are UK taxpayers
- they all sign or have signed a Gift Aid declaration
- you can prove that they have made the payment.

See www.hmrc.gov.uk/charities/gift_aid for more information on Gift Aid.

---

## Three words of caution

1   There are various laws covering fundraising, which mainly concentrate on avoiding theft and misleading the public. There are also specific regulations on lotteries, raffles and tombolas, public collections and using external fundraising consultants. For further information, see the publications listed on pages 128 to 129.

2   In fundraising it is very easy to become funder-led: doing what you think you can raise money for, rather than what you and your users want. Chasing money because it's there may work in the short term; however, after a while the organisation will start to fall apart as people drift away, saying, 'This is not what I got involved for.'

3   Try to strike a balance between scattering your fundraising energies over too many sources and being over-dependent on a single source. You have to have an awful lot of resources if you are to keep a large number of fundraising pots warm; on the other hand, reliance on a single funder can put you right in the funder's pocket.

In general, in your fundraising try to build on your current strengths and successes. If you have a successful annual event, what can you do to make it even better? If you have a key funder, what are you doing to maintain and develop your relationship so that it bears fruit for many years to come? Or are you just assuming – or hoping – that this will continue to go well?

- Fundraising is simple, but not easy. It is not rocket science; don't be seduced by fancy jargon. However, it is often a lot of hard work and you need to make sure that the work is done.
- Fundraising is friend-raising. Relationships are the key. The more personal your fundraising, the more effective it will be.

# Managing your assets

The other side of getting resources is making the most of what you already have. Your organisation's assets fall under five headings: equipment, property, stock, cash and investments.

## Equipment

You must make sure that all your organisation's equipment is properly recorded. This asset register should list all your equipment, giving details of date of purchase, supplier, purchase price, warranties and maintenance agreement.

Equipment should be properly serviced, maintained and insured. People using it should be properly trained, and health and safety regulations enforced.

## Property

Any property that you own or rent must be kept in good condition and insured. Also, if you are letting out space, make sure that you are receiving the best possible returns.

## Stock

If you keep stocks of goods for sale, such as publications or merchandise, make sure that:

- there is a system for keeping records of stock
- all stock is safely and securely stored
- it is fully insured
- the quantity is in line with what you expect to sell, and is not out of date
- you keep an accurate record of stock values.

## Cash

You should be receiving maximum interest on the cash you hold. You need to:

- know where cash is held, in what sort of accounts (current, bank deposit, building society), the interest you earn and the charges you pay
- have a system to move cash balances to interest-bearing accounts as quickly as possible
- make sure you have access to money placed in high-yielding accounts when you are likely to need it.

## Investments

If you have large cash balances, look at the high-interest options, including the money markets. Charity Bank has money deposit schemes specifically for charities (see *Useful addresses*, page 124).

However, unlike a commercial company, a charity is limited in its investment powers. Your constitution may further limit what you can do. In any case you must be very careful to spread the risk across a range of investments and regularly review your investment performance so as to minimise risk and maximise returns.

# And finally...

Once again, trustees need to keep a balance between time and responsibilities, between governance and management. If you become too heavily involved in fundraising activities (and this is easily done) you won't have enough time for the important strategic and policy decisions. However, there's no point in having a marvellous business plan and no cash to finance it. By spreading the load, and through appropriate delegation, the management committee should be able to ensure that all bases are covered. Just because there is a lot to do, especially on the fundraising side, it doesn't mean that you as an individual trustee have to try to do it all.

# 11 Being accountable

Accountability is a key concept for charities. A person or organisation becomes accountable when powers or resources are delegated to them. They have to account for the way in which they use them. Accountability flows in different directions. If you delegate to someone else he or she becomes accountable to you. But as a charity trustee you are held to account for the conduct and activities of your organisation.

Unless there is a real need for confidentiality, you should always be ready to explain and justify the policies you have chosen to adopt. Charities are expected to be open in their dealings, with their donors, with their members, staff and volunteers, with the public and with the Charity Commission.

## Different types of accountability

Donors give money to a charity to undertake certain work or to achieve certain things. The trustees are accountable to the donors for how the money is spent.

In a membership organisation, the management committee has power delegated by the membership to govern the organisation in accordance with the constitution. The committee is accountable to its membership.

All charitable organisations are expected to work for the general public good – public benefit, as the Charity Commission terms it. In return, they receive tax and other advantages. Charities are delegated power by the general public to work on their behalf. They are therefore accountable to the public, which includes the requirement to send their full accounts to anyone who asks for them in writing.

Registered charities must account for their activities to the Charity Commission. This includes sending their annual report and accounts to the Commission, plus completing an annual return (for further information on the different accounting requirements for different organisations, see *Understanding your finances*, page 49).

# The annual report

One of the key ways of accounting for your actions to all your different constituencies is through your annual report. Many people regard producing the annual report as a chore, but it can be a vital marketing and publicity tool. Too few organisations make full use of their annual report, so it is worth giving it serious thought. (For more details, consult *How to Produce Inspiring Annual Reports* – see page 130.)

If you are a charity, there are certain legal aspects to your annual report. It should account for:

- your financial affairs
- your progress in pursuing your aims
- your effectiveness in achieving your objects
- the key people involved (management committee and senior staff).

However, the fact that the report needs to contain certain information doesn't mean it has to be dull. A good annual report will:

- include a brief statement of your overall aims and mission
- contain brief, enthusiastic reports on your organisation's work and achievements during the year (remember: you won't be able to say everything, so say what is most interesting and relevant to your readers).
- include relevant facts and figures, case studies or descriptions which capture the quality of your activities or services
- assess progress over the year, highlighting achievements and reflecting on key challenges
- contain photographs and diagrams, not just words
- use short paragraphs and sub-headings to break up long portions of text
- use pie charts or summaries of financial information, rather than a full set of accounts
- be lively and readable so that it will be noticed and read.

Although the management committee is ultimately responsible for the report, you are unlikely to achieve the best results if you try to write it as a committee. Delegate responsibility to one person, who should have a clear timetable and procedure, allowing for comments and contributions from trustees at the appropriate point.

Many organisations, especially the larger ones, are now producing annual reviews as well as annual reports. The annual review is basically the annual report but without the boring bits: containing things such as key aims, key achievements in the year, interesting stories, major events, a financial summary (ideally with visuals such as pie charts rather than lots of text), basic contact details and laced throughout with pictures. You can't produce an annual review *instead* of an annual report – your annual report is a legal requirement. But if you think the annual report is getting too long and too complicated then try also producing a shorter, punchier annual review. The above guidelines apply to an annual review just as much as an annual report.

## Other ways of reporting

The annual report alone may not be enough to ensure that everyone is kept informed. You may also need to:

- produce simple leaflets or brochures for wider circulation
- get on local radio and in newspapers.

> *I never realised how easy it is to get on local radio until I did my first press release for the project. The local weekly paper reproduced it word for word at the bottom of a column somewhere, but the local radio station called me in to do a live interview. It seemed to me that they were quite desperate for content.*

- hold open meetings with members, users and beneficiaries
- produce formal reports according to set criteria for official funders such as a local authority or the Big Lottery Fund
- report in person to key people (such as major donors).

In general, you should be looking to see that the organisation is promoted effectively and that this is done in keeping with its aims and values.

## Reporting to funders

Many funders make it a condition of their grant that they receive your annual report and accounts, plus a more detailed report on how you have spent their money. They like these reports to concentrate on outputs and achievements. In jargon terms they like to know about:

- *inputs* – what goes into the organisation, the resources and effort the organisation spends on its different activities
- *processes* – how the work is done
- *outputs* – the short-term achievements, numbers of people benefiting, targets met
- *outcomes* – the longer-term impact of the work done in meeting a need, solving a problem, creating change.

*Inputs* and *processes* relate to what the people in your organisation do and the way they do it. *Outputs* relate to what the organisation does for its users and beneficiaries. *Outcomes* show what impact you have made on the needs you set out to tackle. You should concentrate on your achievements in terms of outputs and outcomes, especially on evidence from your users and beneficiaries that they are happy with what you do and how you do it.

## Accountability to users

Your users or beneficiaries are key voices in your planning, monitoring and reporting of processes. It is not enough simply to decide what you think your users might want and then go full steam ahead. Your funders, members and supporters will all want to know that the people you exist to help are happy with what you are doing. There are various ways of receiving feedback:

* using surveys and questionnaires
* conducting interviews
* setting up monitoring groups where trustees, staff and users discuss progress
* having users on the management committee.

It is always worth having positive quotes or testimonies from users in publicity material.

## Staff and volunteers

There is a two-way accountability process between staff and trustees. First, the staff and volunteers are responsible to the management committee, which has delegated certain tasks to them but which remains responsible for all the organisation's activities. There are a number of ways of monitoring this:

* Receiving reports at management committee meetings – it is usual for the chief executive to present a report on progress and events since the last meeting; you may wish to receive additional reports from individual departments or on particular activities.
* Setting up steering or sub-committees to oversee particular aspects of the organisation's work and development.
* Talking to staff, volunteers and service users.
* Visiting projects or activities to see the work at first hand. A measure of tact is needed to ensure that staff and volunteers feel you are genuinely interested in their work and take your responsibilities

seriously, but that you are not trying to do their job for them. The boundary between governance and management can often become blurred in small organisations.

It is equally important that staff and volunteers feel part of things; that their ideas and actions count and are valued. You should make sure that management committee decisions are communicated to the staff – including, where possible, the reasons behind them. You also need to ensure that staff have proper supervision and support and that they feel the management committee is pulling its weight (see *Understanding your staff and volunteers*, page 41).

## Members and supporters

If you are a membership organisation, you will have to account to your members formally at your annual general meeting and informally through newsletters and other publicity material.

Annual general meetings are sometimes seen as unfortunate legal necessities, or as opportunities for people to meddle unnecessarily in the affairs of the charity. However, it is much better to use them as opportunities to celebrate the past year, look forward to the opportunities and challenges ahead and, in general, galvanise, enthuse and re-motivate the organisation. It is important that the chair's report sets a positive and constructive tone, and that all members of the management committee are on hand to meet and hear from the organisation's members and supporters.

Newsletters are good ways of keeping in touch with members. As with your annual report (see page 68), keep them lively and upbeat, maybe inviting views and contributions from members, supporters, staff, volunteers and key contacts. They don't need to be glossily produced, although they should appear consistent with the values and status of your organisation. Make sure that you keep an eye on all the costs involved, from design, print and production through to time spent on putting them together and sending them out: newsletters can become a problematic drain on organisational resources as well as a terrific asset.

Websites, email, Facebook, Twitter and whatever else emerges over the lifetime of this book will also offer possibilities for keeping in touch with members and supporters. The general rule is to try and keep things as opt-in as possible and ensure that you keep communication focused and timely. There is a real danger that just because in a sense email is free and the post isn't, that all rules about how and when you contact actual or potential supporters are forgotten in a barrage of regular and apparently indiscriminate emails that clog up the recipient's in box. There are plenty of opportunities to get electronic communication right, but this kind of thoughtlessness is as good a way as any to alienate your support base.

## And finally . . .

In general, you should aim to be as open as possible in your dealings with people and monitoring organisations. Obviously, you will have confidential information that it would be inappropriate to discuss and there may be discussions going on (say over strategy) that for the time being are best kept private. That is a matter for your judgement. But as a rule it is better to involve people rather than exclude them.

# PART **THREE**

# Getting the work done

# 12 Organising your meetings

As a trustee you have a number of responsibilities and a lot of work to get through. Management committees must meet together to make decisions, share information and ensure that the organisation is being effectively managed. However, you do not have unlimited time, so committee members need to work effectively together to complete the tasks required in the allotted time.

The management committee is responsible for running itself. One of the most important aspects of this is ensuring that you hold effective meetings. There are various ways of doing this, and you need to choose the method which best suits you. However, you should bear the following points in mind:

- The committee as a whole is responsible for making meetings effective. It is a team effort.
- The chair has an important role in meetings, but is one among many, and relies on the positive contribution of all members.
- The agenda is the main tool for organising the meeting. Like all tools it can be used well, or abused.
- A relaxed climate in which all trustees feel able to participate is essential.
- Members must observe proper standards of confidentiality.
- Members must feel committed to, and work co-operatively for the organisation as a whole.

> Working through Checklist 3, *Information, communication and decision making* (see page 102), will provide you with some more useful pointers on this topic.

## Why hold meetings?

Your constitution will require the management committee to hold a certain number of meetings a year. However, meetings are not just about fulfilling your legal responsibilities. You also hold meetings to:

- decide the strategy and policies for the organisation
- agree objectives, priorities and plans

- receive information to monitor progress
- solve problems
- make decisions on what needs to be done and who should do it
- ratify decisions made elsewhere (for example, by sub-committees)
- share views and opinions
- educate committee members about the work of the organisation and the issues that affect it
- provide support and social contact between committee members.

You can't do all of the above all of the time, so committee members need to be aware of the purpose of each part of the meeting.

You should guard against allowing the management committee to become bogged down in administrative detail. For example, there may be an agenda item to decide on the purchase of a computer. The committee should be clear about why there is a need for a computer (this may be to hold membership details, to do the accounts, or whatever) and take a decision accordingly. However, it should not try to choose which computer to buy. Leave that to a member of staff or delegate it to an individual trustee. Keep the committee's eye on the bigger picture.

## When do you hold meetings?

Your constitution will require you to hold a minimum number of meetings a year. However, in most organisations you will need to meet more frequently. It is up to each organisation to decide how often is appropriate. As a general rule, if you are meeting fewer than four times a year, the management committee will become sidelined and powerless; if you are meeting more than once a month the management committee is doing too much and should delegate more.

Some organisations adopt a system of regular meetings of the whole committee (say six times a year) and interim meetings of one or more sub-committees to keep an eye on particular areas of operation.

## The agenda

The main tool for organising your meetings is the agenda, as this sets out the plan for the meeting. It is much more than just a list of headings. Each agenda item should tell management committee members exactly what will be discussed and why, so that they can prepare properly for the meeting.

There are five main reasons why an item may be on the agenda for the meeting:

- to report – to give information, ideas or opinions to the meeting
- to consult – to obtain information, ideas or opinions from people at the meeting
- to discuss – to talk about an issue or problem, but without coming to a conclusion or decision at that meeting
- to resolve a problem – to hear as much as possible about a particular problem and come to a conclusion about how to deal with such difficulties, but without necessarily deciding to take specific action now
- to make a decision – to decide to take action about something.

You need to be clear about each item on the agenda. Ask yourself (and, if necessary, others):

- Why is this item on the agenda? What do we want to achieve by considering it?
- If the item is not appropriate for discussion at the management committee, where should it be dealt with?
- Who will be responsible for any action agreed?

Good meetings need good, clear agendas rather than vague lists of discussion topics. It is also important that members stick to the items on the agenda. Otherwise, you will wander all around the houses, achieve nothing, and end up with everyone frustrated and disillusioned.

## Effective committee meetings

The management committee operates through meetings. The best meetings are where people can work together in an atmosphere of trust and commitment to achieve agreed results. An effective committee has:

- the right kind of members, with appropriate skills, experience and knowledge
- a clear and agreed purpose
- a good size (generally between five and fifteen members)
- an effective chair
- a positive atmosphere

> *I actually enjoy committee meetings. I get a real sense of like-minded people pulling together over something they believe in.*

- good administration (agendas and relevant papers)
- good record keeping (minutes)
- confidence that decisions will be implemented – this is key.

Plan social time before or after the meeting. This means that people have the chance to chat in an informal environment and get to know each other better, but without this intruding on the meeting itself. You may not go so far as to have a fully timed agenda, but always have a start and a finish time and don't go for more than 90 minutes without a break.

You may want to set some explicit ground rules, such as:
- It's OK to ask questions.
- If in doubt, ask.
- Keep contributions brief and to the point.
- Don't just repeat other people's contributions.
- Listen to other people's contributions.
- Don't interrupt.
- Don't use jargon and abbreviations unless they are explained.
- Don't text and email during meetings. Put phones and BlackBerrys away and concentrate on the meeting instead.

You will need someone to act as secretary. This can be the same person each time or the task may be done in rotation. Whoever takes the minutes should take care to note all action points, with a name or names next to each one. They should try to summarise the main points of discussion, but there is no need to attempt a verbatim record of everything that was said. (See also *The secretary,* page 82)

# Ineffective committee meetings

It's fairly easy to derail committee meetings through inappropriate behaviour. Try to guard against the following:

*Intimidation* – some people are so sure of their own views and position that they have no time for anyone else's. Alternatively, people may be so attached to their ideas and arguments that they take questions or disagreement as personal criticism.

*Rushing* – it's important to talk things through. What seems a perfectly good and straightforward idea to one person may not be particularly clear or acceptable to another. Also, ideas may have wide-ranging financial implications. Even though it might be really good to adopt a particular course of action, it doesn't mean that you automatically go ahead and do it: you may not be able to afford it.

*Agenda dyslexia* – jumping about, or even off, the agenda. Stick to the matter at hand, even if a discussion about last night's television or world poverty would be more interesting.

*Proceduralism* – using knowledge of committee rules, however obscure, to thwart decisions.

*Nit-picking* – raising obscure points of detail to undermine confidence, even after the decision has been made. You don't have to sort out every last detail before the committee can decide to go ahead.

*Raking over the past* – going back to previous decisions and trying to get them reversed. There may be times when a decision was clearly wrong or proved to be wrong in the light of future events. Fine; that kind of decision needs reviewing. However, don't let that be cover for people just to keep going over and over old ground either because they didn't agree with it (although everyone else did) and want it to be changed, or because they don't want to deal with the matters in hand.

*Negativity* – try not to focus just on the reasons why something might not work, or require yet more information before you make a decision. There will be many occasions when you say, effectively, 'On balance, this seems like a good way ahead.' There may be forceful arguments against, but better ones for doing it.

*Recklessness* – just 'giving it a go', or saying yes because you want to leave on time. Decisions need to be thought through and discussed properly.

As with most things in management committee life, you need to strike a balance between undue caution and reckless optimism; between giving space for and valuing everyone's contribution and allowing the discussion to go round and round in circles; between procrastination and railroading. The chair needs to be particularly vigilant, keeping the meeting positive and moving things forward at an appropriate speed.

## Making decisions

*Committees work best when everyone takes responsibility – rather than leaving everything to the chair – and everyone plays a role. This helps create a positive atmosphere for debate.*

The chair should make sure that:

- members are always clear what decision they are being asked to take
- any views for and against the decision have been heard
- there is clear agreement on the decision – if not, move to a vote
- voting is minuted, so that anyone who disagrees can ask for their disagreement to be recorded

- there is a summing up at the end of each item, noting the decision and action required.

It may be that you cannot reach a decision yet, because you need more information. However, don't use this as an excuse to avoid making hard choices.

In general, you have to steer a course between efficiency and decision-making on the one hand, and sensitivity and inclusiveness on the other. If one or two dominant committee members simply railroad decisions through meetings, the remaining trustees will become disillusioned and drift away – or at best only make a minimal contribution. Equally, decisions have to be taken, even when not everyone agrees.

## Staff attendance at committee meetings

The paid employees of a charity are not generally allowed, by law, to be voting members of its management committee. However, staff can take part in discussions and their attendance can help relationships and communication between committee and staff. The management committee can always ask for staff members to leave the meeting if they want to discuss matters privately.

In smaller organisations, with only two or three staff, it can be helpful for all members of staff to attend management committee meetings to speed up the information flow and build a sense of joint working. In larger organisations, this is impossible.

The most senior staff member usually attends meetings. Other staff members can either attend regularly because of their role (for instance, the finance manager may need to provide information to the treasurer and committee), or attend by invitation to discuss matters of particular relevance to their work. Large organisations often involve the whole of their senior management team in management committee meetings.

## And finally . . .

Much of your trusteeship will revolve around meetings, especially management committee meetings. Try to make sure, as far as possible, that the meetings are well structured so that you can make a valuable contribution while listening to the views of others, and that the decisions you make reflect the combined wisdom, experience and expertise of the whole committee.

# 13 Special roles on the management committee

Although all trustees are responsible for everything that goes on, there are three key bases to cover: namely those of chair, secretary and treasurer. Even if you don't use all these titles (not every voluntary organisation has a treasurer, for example), you need to ensure that the functions are well covered.

## The chair

The chair has to ensure that the management committee functions properly, that everyone is able to contribute fully during the meetings, that all the items on the agenda are discussed and that effective decisions are made. The position of chair is difficult but key. The chair is expected to provide leadership, but must not dominate the meeting or inhibit other members' contributions. They must also know the rules for the conduct of meetings, as set down in the governing instrument.

And it is not simply a question of chairing meetings. The role of the chair includes:

- being a figurehead of the organisation. This will often include representing the organisation at other meetings, speaking on its behalf and attending public functions
- making sure that the management committee operates effectively, that it is made up of suitable, active and committed members with the appropriate mix of skills and experience to run the organisation
- ensuring appropriate supervision of staff. The chair often directly supervises the senior member of staff in the organisation
- assisting with the management of the organisation. The chair may find her/himself involved in some of the managerial tasks of the organisation. This could involve overseeing budgets and expenditure, signing cheques, liaising with the treasurer, signing letters and participating in staff recruitment.

Acting as a chair can be a time-consuming business. It is important that the person chosen has the time as well as the skills to bring to the role.

*Our chair is a lecturer at the university. Although she seems to put in incredibly long hours, her timetable is pretty flexible, so she's generally available for meetings, even at short notice. And the political skills she's developed in academic meetings are just what's needed to keep our rather eccentric bunch of trustees in order!*

# The secretary

Most constitutions require that there is a secretary to the trustees. In organisations with paid staff, secretarial duties can be delegated to a staff member. Where there are no paid staff, the secretary is an important and time-consuming role for a trustee or volunteer.

A key task is minute taking. The minutes are a legal record of the decisions taken by the management committee. They are checked by all committee members and, once approved, signed at the next meeting by the chair. The decisions are legally binding.

Minutes should give a clear, accurate record of decisions taken. They are not full transcripts of the meeting. Rather, they:

- summarise the key points made in discussion
- record decisions taken
- identify what actions were agreed, who is responsible for doing the work and by when.

Each set of minutes should also include the date of the meeting, a full list of who was present and when the meeting started and finished. When summarising discussions, don't include names or personal references unless there is a particular reason for doing so – for example, when a trustee wants to record opposition to a decision. (For more information see *The Minute Taker's Handbook* – details on page 131.)

Some organisations ask a non-trustee to be minutes secretary, as this frees all trustees to take a full part in the meeting. If this is the case, the secretary will not have all the responsibilities listed below, so the chair may have to take on some or all of these instead.

Other tasks of the secretary include:

- keeping a check on the progress of the work agreed by the management committee

- ensuring that the organisation meets its legal obligations, including reporting to the Charity Commission and meeting charity law requirements checking that there is a quorum at meetings (your constitution will require a minimum number of members to be in attendance before a meeting is legally valid – this minimum number is called a quorum)
- making arrangements for the meetings (booking the room, arranging refreshments and so on)
- preparing the agenda (with the chair)
- circulating the agenda with papers and previous minutes well in advance of the meeting
- checking that members have followed through agreed action since the last meeting
- keeping a list of trustees, plus their postal and email addresses and telephone numbers
- ensuring that members are informed of annual general meetings and any special meetings
- maintaining records of correspondence.

The job of secretary can be demanding, especially for someone who is not very well organised. It can be one of those jobs that you only really notice when things go wrong; but where it is well done, it can relieve the chair of a considerable administrative burden.

*I've been a PA for 20 years. I had a really solid, traditional secretarial training – including shorthand! I'm not very good at speaking in public, and I felt I wasn't contributing much to meetings, so I was relieved when they asked me to be secretary.*

## The treasurer

The treasurer's job is to monitor the organisation's finances on behalf of the whole committee, to report regularly on them to the committee, and to make sure that money and property are properly managed. The treasurer does not necessarily do all the book-keeping, record-keeping, budgeting and such like, but needs to make sure that they are done and done properly. This requires:

- proper systems for budgeting, financial control and reporting to be in place
- procedures to reduce the risk of fraud
- all trustees to be kept properly informed about the state of the organisation's finances

- financial reports to the trustees that are comprehensible and properly discussed
- accounts and other financial reports to be produced in the proper form and on time as required by other bodies (such as the Charity Commission)
- competent auditors or an independent examiner to be appointed, according to legal requirements (see page 50).

But even if you have a treasurer, remember that all trustees are responsible for the organisation's finances and for getting sufficient financial information about the organisation.

# 14 Delegation

Ultimate responsibility for running a voluntary organisation rests with the management committee as a whole. However, there can be a lot of work to get through, and you may want to spread the load by having others take on different bits of the workload.

*It is vital to have a sense of shared responsibility, of having common goals, instead of a 'them and us' attitude. We need to recognise that people have diverse skills and make sure that we use these skills creatively in the team.*

You can delegate tasks to individual committee members (such as appointing a treasurer to oversee the finances), to sub-committees, working groups, managers, staff, volunteers or specialist advisers. However, always remember:

- although you can delegate the task, you cannot delegate legal responsibility – everything that the charity does ultimately comes down to you, even if you are not aware of what is being done
- delegation can lead to confusion about who is supposed to be doing what – you need to provide a clear brief so that people know what is expected of them.

## Sub-committees

The management committee of a small organisation can usually carry out most of the business itself, and does not need to delegate work to sub-committees. However, as the organisation becomes more complex it may be helpful to set up small committees with delegated powers to carry out particular roles.

Typical sub-committees include:

- finance committee – to oversee the financial affairs of the organisation
- finance and general purposes committee – to oversee financial, general staffing and management matters; this committee often meets between management committee meetings to keep an eye on things generally
- audit committee – to oversee the annual audit and ensure that all recommendations are followed through

- fundraising committee – to oversee the fundraising strategy and organise fundraising events
- staff committee – to oversee staff management and development
- project committee – to oversee the work of a particular project or development.

A key feature of sub-committees is that they are set up to be ongoing and are part of the formal structure of the organisation (shorter-term committees tend to be called working groups – see *Working groups*, page 86). The chair of each sub-committee is usually a trustee and therefore sits on the main management committee. This helps to ensure clear lines of communication (see *Maintaining communication*, page 88).

The main advantages of sub-committees are that they:

- are focused on a small range of tasks
- can recruit members with particular expertise or experience
- can involve staff members in areas relevant to their work.

The main disadvantages tend to be:

- communication between them and the management committee can break down
- they can be seen as powerful cliques – the place where the real decisions are made before being rubber-stamped by the management committee
- they require even more time from management committee members
- their roles may not be clearly defined and can overlap with the remit of other committees, causing confusion and duplication
- they may want more independence and freedom of action than the management committee is prepared to give them
- they may cease to have a valid purpose, but continue to meet in any case
- individual committee members see it as 'their' committee and are difficult to remove.

Each sub-committee must therefore always have its own, very clear brief (see *Providing a clear brief*, page 88).

# Working groups

A working group is less formal than a sub-committee. It is set up to deal with a particular task or issue. It has a limited lifespan and is dissolved when it has completed its work.

Many of the advantages and disadvantages of working groups are the same as those for sub-committees. One difference is that working groups tend to include a much higher proportion of staff and volunteers; this means they can become a forum either for positive debate and engagement, or for moaning and complaint.

Working groups are often set up to look at issues such as:

- equal opportunities or anti-racism policies
- feasibility studies (for example, moving to new premises)
- specific problem areas (such as staff development opportunities)
- organisational structures
- the implications of new legislation.

For example, an equal opportunities working group may be asked to:

- review the organisation's equal opportunities policy in the light of current legislation and best practice
- assess significant areas of weakness or under-representation among management committee, staff, volunteers and service users
- assess how the organisation promotes and publicises itself and its activities from an equal opportunities perspective.

Having done this, the group may be asked to draft:

- a revised statement of intent on equal opportunities, outlining the organisation's commitment to equal opportunities
- a revised code of practice, outlining how the organisation will implement equal opportunities in relation to the recruitment and selection of management committee members, staff and volunteers; conditions of employment and volunteering; the recruitment of members and users; the provision and publicising of services and activities.

Alongside this, it could also be asked to:

- highlight and prioritise key decisions and actions that need to be taken
- propose ways of monitoring progress in these crucial areas.

Working groups generally have fewer decision-making powers than subcommittees; their role is more advisory. However, it is important to spell this out in advance, to avoid frustration and disappointment later.

# Providing a clear brief

Much confusion can arise in the delegation process if it is not clear exactly what is being delegated. Job descriptions play a vital role in clarifying what is being entrusted to a particular individual. In the case of a committee, is it just being asked to provide information to help management committee members make a decision? Or is it supposed to be putting forward proposals or recommendations to the management committee, or even taking the decision itself? It can be tricky reining in a committee once it has exceeded its powers; it can be even more difficult overturning a decision that has been unilaterally taken and announced by a sub-committee when the management committee was expecting to discuss the matter itself.

Therefore, whenever a committee is set up it should have a clear brief (often called terms of reference). This brief should spell out:

- the purpose of the committee or working group – what it is aiming to achieve and what results are wanted
- the powers of action (plus the limits to these powers) and the decision making delegated to the committee – whether decisions need to be ratified by the management committee
- how long the group is there for – whether it is permanent or has a limited lifespan
- how and when it should report back to the management committee
- who should be on the committee, and why
- how they should be appointed
- how often the committee should meet
- the role of the chair and minute taker in meetings
- who receives copies of the minutes
- who convenes the meetings.

People need to know exactly what they are expected to do when they join a sub-committee or working group. Only then can they decide whether they have the time, interest and expertise to make a worthwhile contribution. If they don't, there is no point in them being there.

# Maintaining communication

Good communication between the management committee and the sub-committee – or person with the delegated authority – is vital. With sub-committees or working groups this is usually a question of reading minutes and/or receiving reports at management committee meetings.

The appointment of the chair of the committee is also key, both in terms of the communication process and to keep the committee focused on the task(s) in hand.

There are various ways in which staff should report to the management committee about tasks delegated to them. A committee meeting should always include a chief executive's report, summarising the main events and developments since the last meeting. The committee may also request other staff members to report on particular projects or areas of activity. However, much of the rest of the reporting will be more indirect, through appraisals and supervision sessions conducted by staff (see *Understanding your staff and volunteers*, page 41).

# And finally...

In general, you need to think about how you spread the management load. The management committee may not be able to do everything. Also, joining an over-burdened and frustrated management committee is hardly an attractive prospect for a potential newcomer. So think about breaking down the organisation's activities into manageable tasks that can be delegated, and then work out the most appropriate structure for doing this. However, always remember to keep control – because the management committee is the one that will have to answer for everything that is done in the name of the organisation.

# PART FOUR

# Getting the most out of being a trustee

# 15 **Pulling it all together**

You are under no formal obligation to enjoy being a trustee. You can be as miserable as you like (and some are!). However, you should find that trusteeship is rewarding. Although there are certain things the committee can do to make sure its members are satisfied, such as giving proper back-up and support, the following is a basic guide to getting the most from your trusteeship.

> Checklist 6, *Personal effectiveness*, page 109 provides a summary of the points you should work through if you want to make the most of your role as trustee.

## Know what is expected of you

Make sure you understand what being on the management committee involves, both in principle (understanding your responsibilities and liabilities) and in practice (forming a realistic picture of what the charity expects from you). You don't want to end up agreeing to do something, only to find that you haven't either the time or the skills to play the role expected of you.

## Don't worry unnecessarily about your liabilities

Take your role seriously, but don't spend your whole time worrying about your liabilities if things go wrong. Take a balanced view and evaluate any risks carefully. But don't let the organisation grind down through a constant fear that something may go wrong. If you've evaluated the risk and on balance it seems a good move, then do it.

## Get to know the other trustees

Try to build up a good working knowledge of the skills and experience that the other members of the committee bring to the work. Try to build trust and rapport with your fellow trustees although, because trustees meet fairly infrequently, this can take time. Social time before or after the meeting can be really helpful.

# Keep informed about the work of the organisation

Keep in touch with what is going on. If possible, visit the organisation reasonably regularly and chat with staff, volunteers and beneficiaries. This should help keep you in touch with the needs that the organisation is trying to meet and with the values and spirit within the organisation. You should also derive a lot of satisfaction from seeing the work being done well and appreciated; this is what you as a management committee member are trying to promote.

# If in doubt, ask

You need to be well informed. If you are unclear about anything, ask. No question is too obvious or too basic.

# Know where to go for information and advice

There will be a good deal of knowledge inside the organisation and on the management committee. You will also have professional advisers (lawyers, accountants and so on). There are also agencies, such as local councils for voluntary service, which exist to help and advise local voluntary organisations (see *Useful addresses*, page 121).

# Don't become overloaded with details

Your main job is to keep a clear overview of the affairs of the organisation, its strategy and development. Don't become bogged down in day-to-day details. Delegate these to sub-committees, working groups and staff. Remember the distinction between governance and management.

# Take an interest in a particular area

Try to develop an interest in an area of the organisation's activities. Give time to a sub-committee or working group or develop an area of specialist knowledge. You might even do some volunteer work for the organisation in addition to your trusteeship. This will not only bring you into contact with fellow trustees and staff members, it will help you feel that you are making a special contribution.

## Be prepared

Make sure that you allocate enough time to read minutes and committee papers before meetings, and make a note of areas where you want more information or that you are particularly concerned about. It's not good enough to flick through papers during the meeting to try and work out what on earth everyone is talking about.

## Follow things through

If you agree to do something, make sure you do it and within an agreed timescale. There is nothing more frustrating for management committees than when its members agree courses of action which are then simply not followed through.

## Set priorities for your work

You know your interests and skills. Give priority to those areas which make best use of them. Avoid the temptation to say 'yes' to everything. You have limited time, so make sure that you and the organisation get the best from it.

## Go to meetings

This may seem a statement of the obvious. However, it is the central point of your commitment, and it is massively de-motivating for your fellow trustees if they feel that they are the only ones making an effort to attend meetings. In any case, you are responsible for all the decisions taken at the meeting whether or not you were in attendance.

## Review your work as a committee member

Ask yourself periodically whether you are still enjoying your trusteeship, whether you are being used most effectively, or even whether it is time to move on.

## Reclaim out-of-pocket expenses

You give your valuable time free to the organisation. You should not be expected to bear the out-of-pocket costs you incur. The management committee should make sure that it has clear, simple and quick systems for repaying committee members' out-of-pocket expenses.

## Pat yourself on the back occasionally

You have decided to give your time voluntarily to something you believe in. Make sure that you recognise and value your contribution, because you are helping the organisation do something really worthwhile in the lives of its beneficiaries or the community.

## And finally...

Your work as a trustee matters. It makes a real difference. Enjoy it!

# Checklists

## Making your management committee and its committees more effective

These checklists will help you improve the effectiveness of your management committee and its sub-committees. Don't be depressed if there is a lot you could be doing better. Choose a few points which seem most important, and start with them. In six months' time, go through the checklists again, see how much you have progressed, and choose a few more improvements. And remember to celebrate what you are doing well.

## Checklist 1: The legal and management framework

Do all members of the management committee receive a copy of the governing document (constitution, trust deed or memorandum of association) as soon as they join, with (if necessary) a summary of the key points or points that are difficult to understand?

Yes ☐　　No ☐

Do members of the management committee know whether our legal structure is an unincorporated association, trust, company limited by guarantee, charitable incorporated organisation (CIO) or industrial and provident society (IPS)?

Yes ☐　　No ☐

If the organisation is a membership organisation (association, company, CIO or IPS), do we understand the difference between the members of the organisation and the members of the management committee?

Yes ☐　　No ☐

Are we absolutely clear about who is on our management committee as a full (voting) member, and who does not have voting rights?

Yes ☐　　No ☐

Do members of the management committee know whether we have charitable status?

Yes ☐　　No ☐

If we are charitable, have all management committee members received a copy of the Charity Commission booklet *The Essential Trustee: What You Need to Know* (CC3)?

Yes ☐　　No ☐

If people are on a sub-committee, do they know who the management committee members are and how they are accountable to the management committee?

Yes ☐　　No ☐

If we have sub-committees, is it clear what decisions they can and can't make?

Yes ☐　　No ☐

© Sandy Adirondack 2010, www.sandy-a.co.uk.
Photocopiable document. Consent required to reproduce or store electronically.

Do new management committee and sub-committee members get an induction pack containing background information about the organisation, its finances and funding and current issues, along with minutes of the past two management committee or sub-committee meetings?

Yes ☐    No ☐

Do we have a library of basic voluntary sector management and governance publications, available to management committee and sub-committee members and staff?

Yes ☐    No ☐

Do management committee members have access to training about the organisation's work and service users, and the financial, legal and management aspects of voluntary sector governance?

Yes ☐    No ☐

Do members of the management committee each take responsibility for learning about one or more aspects of governance and acting as a 'lead person' for the management committee and staff on that issue? (Topics might include employment contractual issues, staff supervision, volunteering, equal opportunities, premises, health and safety, data protection, finance, funding, fundraising, charity law, company law, insurances, publicity and various aspects of your organisation's services.)

Yes ☐    No ☐

**Highlight or circle the items ticked 'no' where your management committee needs to take action.**

© Sandy Adirondack 2010, www.sandy-a.co.uk.
Photocopiable document. Consent required to reproduce or store electronically.

## Checklist 2: Governance

Do management committee and sub-committee members know what the organisation's objects are as set out in our governing document?

Yes ☐    No ☐

Do management committee members understand what is meant by conflict of interest and conflict of loyalties and how they apply to them, do we have procedures for disclosure of such conflicts, and do we have a register of interests where these are recorded?

Yes ☐    No ☐

Do we regularly discuss the ethos or values which underpin our work?

Yes ☐    No ☐

Are management committee and sub-committee members aware of how our activities, services and campaigns further our objects and reflect our values?

Yes ☐    No ☐

Do we regularly consult our members, service users and others concerned with our organisation about how they would like us to develop?

Yes ☐    No ☐

Do we have a strategic plan, setting out how we want to develop over the next two to three years (for a small organisation) or three to ten years or more (for a larger organisation)?

Yes ☐    No ☐

Do we have a process for carrying out an annual review of our overall work and for setting defined objectives or targets for the next year or two?

Yes ☐    No ☐

Do we have proper procedures for assessing and reducing the risks faced by the organisation (e.g. fire, flood, theft, health and safety, finance, legal and contractual compliance, information, reputation)?

Yes ☐    No ☐

© Sandy Adirondack 2010, www.sandy-a.co.uk.
Photocopiable document. Consent required to reproduce or store electronically.

Do the management committee and sub-committees regularly receive reports from employees and/or volunteers about their work, progress, problems and plans, and how they are achieving the targets set out in the strategic plan and annual review?

Yes ☐    No ☐

**Highlight or circle the items ticked 'no' where your management committee needs to take action.**

© Sandy Adirondack 2010, www.sandy-a.co.uk.
Photocopiable document. Consent required to reproduce or store electronically.

## Checklist 3: Information, communication and decision making

Do we get good agendas for meetings, setting out clearly the items to be covered, who will introduce each item, and whether each item is for information, discussion or decision?

Yes ☐   No ☐

Do we get proper written information before meetings, with necessary background?

Yes ☐   No ☐

Do management committee and sub-committee meetings start on time, provide opportunities for refreshments, and finish in good time?

Yes ☐   No ☐

Are agenda items properly introduced, so everyone understands the issues?

Yes ☐   No ☐

Does the chair keep the discussion focused, ensure everyone who wants to speak has a reasonable chance to do so, summarise fairly, and help the group reach decisions?

Yes ☐   No ☐

Do all participants act responsibly in meetings: sticking to the point, not personalising issues, not getting abusive, and valuing every person's contribution?

Yes ☐   No ☐

Do the minutes of meetings accurately reflect the decisions made, action required to implement the decisions and main points leading to decisions?

Yes ☐   No ☐

**Highlight or circle the items ticked 'no' where your management committee needs to take action.**

# Checklist 4: Employment and volunteers

Does someone on the management committee and someone on the staff have explicit responsibility for keeping up to date with employment law and with related law such as equal opportunities, health and safety and safeguarding children and vulnerable adults?

Yes ☐　　No ☐

Are management committee members aware of how many employees we employ, how many are full- and part-time, how many are on open contracts and how many on fixed-term contracts, where the funding comes from for each post and how secure it is?

Yes ☐　　No ☐

Do we have good recruitment procedures for employees and volunteers, that we are sure comply with the law and good practice on equal opportunities?

Yes ☐　　No ☐

Do our employees receive, within two months of starting work, written terms and conditions of employment complying with current employment legislation?

Yes ☐　　No ☐

Are management committee members aware of the main points in employees' contracts, e.g. holiday entitlement, sickness, parental entitlements and redundancy pay entitlement?

Yes ☐　　No ☐

Are contracts of employment reviewed at least every two years?

Yes ☐　　No ☐

Do all employees have a written job description, and is it reviewed with the employee at least once a year?

Yes ☐　　No ☐

Do we have a volunteer policy setting out, for example, volunteers' entitlement to training and reimbursement of expenses?

Yes ☐　　No ☐

© Sandy Adirondack 2010, www.sandy-a.co.uk.
Photocopiable document. Consent required to reproduce or store electronically.

If appropriate, do volunteers and trainees have written role descriptions, and are they regularly reviewed?

Yes ☐    No ☐

Do all employees, volunteers and trainees have an induction programme?

Yes ☐    No ☐

Do employees, volunteers and trainees have access to ongoing training?

Yes ☐    No ☐

Do we have a clear management structure so employees, volunteers and trainees know who they are accountable to, and who they should go to if they need information or support?

Yes ☐    No ☐

Do all employees, volunteers and trainees have a regular opportunity to discuss their work progress and problems with a manager, management committee member or other appropriate person?

Yes ☐    No ☐

Does the chief executive/director/senior staff member meet regularly with a management committee member to discuss progress and problems and review the senior staff member's work, and is the management committee kept informed of these discussions?

Yes ☐    No ☐

Are our disciplinary and grievance procedures for employees (including the senior staff member), volunteers and trainees legal and workable, and do we regularly review them?

Yes ☐    No ☐

Do employees, volunteers, trainees and the management committee work in partnership, without any hint of an 'us and them' mentality?

Yes ☐    No ☐

When we use self-employed workers, consultants etc. do we have clear contracts with them setting out what we expect from them, deadlines, how the work will be monitored, how complaints will be dealt with, how payment will be determined and when the person will be paid?

Yes ☐    No ☐

© Sandy Adirondack 2010, www.sandy-a.co.uk.
Photocopiable document. Consent required to reproduce or store electronically.

Before paying anyone on a self-employed (non-PAYE) basis do we take proper steps to ensure we do not have to operate PAYE for them?

Yes ☐      No ☐

**Highlight or circle the items ticked 'no' where your management committee needs to take action.**

© Sandy Adirondack 2010, www.sandy-a.co.uk.
Photocopiable document. Consent required to reproduce or store electronically.

## Checklist 5: Finance

Does our treasurer understand that he or she is responsible for overseeing our finances on behalf of the whole management committee, and must regularly report to it?

Yes ☐    No ☐

Does our treasurer have a level of financial awareness and skill appropriate to our organisation?

Yes ☐    No ☐

Does the treasurer oversee the work of the finance director or finance worker(s)?

Yes ☐    No ☐

Do we have procedures to reduce the risk of fraud, e.g. all cheques signed by two people, proper procedures for authorising telephone or electronic transactions, no one can sign a cheque or authorise a payment to themselves or a relative, all cash takings must be counted with another person, all petty cash payments must be authorised and signed for?

Yes ☐    No ☐

Do we have procedures in place to ensure money is as secure as possible, e.g. keeping the absolute minimum cash on the premises, and keeping it secure?

Yes ☐    No ☐

Does the management committee agree budgets? Are the budgets realistic?

Yes ☐    No ☐

Do the finance sub-committee (if there is one) and management committee receive regular financial reports setting out income and expenditure for the year to date, set against budgeted income and expenditure, with an explanation of any significant variance between actual and budget?

Yes ☐    No ☐

Do the financial reports also show our current financial position: not only how much we have in the bank or investments, but also how much we owe and how much we are owed?

Yes ☐    No ☐

© Sandy Adirondack 2010, www.sandy-a.co.uk.
Photocopiable document. Consent required to reproduce or store electronically.

Are management committee members aware of whether the organisation's accounts must be audited or examined by an independent person, each year? (This requirement could arise from charity law, company or IPS law, funders, and/or the organisation's governing document.)

Yes ☐    No ☐

Are management committee members provided with training to ensure they can understand the financial reports, annual accounts and the organisation's overall financial situation?

Yes ☐    No ☐

Has the management committee agreed – and does it regularly review – its policy on reserves, ensuring that adequate reserves are kept to ensure the organisation can continue operating or, if necessary, wind down properly?

Yes ☐    No ☐

Has the management committee agreed – and does it regularly review – its policy on investments? (This includes not only stocks and shares, but also money kept in interest-earning accounts.)

Yes ☐    No ☐

If the organisation owns furniture, equipment, vehicles or other assets, does it keep an asset register (a list of assets, when purchased or received and value)?

Yes ☐    No ☐

If the organisation holds stock waiting to be used or sold, does it do regular stock checks, and are procedures in place to reduce pilferage or damage?

Yes ☐    No ☐

Is the organisation incorporated as a company limited by guarantee, charitable incorporated organisation (CIO) or industrial and provident society (IPS)?

Yes ☐    No ☐

If it is not incorporated and has employees, a lease, property, long-term contracts and/or insecure funding, is it considering incorporation?

Yes ☐    No ☐

© Sandy Adirondack 2010, www.sandy-a.co.uk.
Photocopiable document. Consent required to reproduce or store electronically.

Does the management committee receive a report at least once a year setting out the insurances the organisation has (and does not have), with recommendations for changes?

Yes ☐    No ☐

Does the management committee review its financial procedures and controls at least once a year, using a checklist such as the Charity Commission's *Internal Financial Controls for Charities* (CC8)?

Yes ☐    No ☐

**Highlight or circle the items ticked 'no' where your management committee needs to take action.**

# Checklist 6: Personal effectiveness

When I get papers for management committee or sub-committee meetings, do I always read them before the meeting?

Yes ☐    No ☐

Do I make a note on the papers of any questions or points I want to raise?

Yes ☐    No ☐

If I know I will want to raise matters which are not on the agenda, do I notify the office or chair before the meeting?

Yes ☐    No ☐

> Even better, does the organisation have a clear process for management committee or sub-committee members and others to get items onto the agenda?
>
> Yes ☐    No ☐

Do I make every possible effort to get to meetings on time?

Yes ☐    No ☐

If I know I am going to be absent or late, do I always notify the office, chair, secretary or other appropriate person (unless I am stuck on the train without a mobile phone)?

Yes ☐    No ☐

If I arrive early, do I make a point of talking to new people or people I don't know very well?

Yes ☐    No ☐

During discussions, do I listen to what people are saying, rather than half-listening while framing my own response, making comments to neighbours or dreaming about getting home and watching TV?

Yes ☐    No ☐

> If you answered 'yes', are you *sure* you really listen? Many people don't.

Do I genuinely respect and value other people's views?

Yes ☐    No ☐

If I disagree with a point, do I always present my views calmly, clearly and rationally, without getting bombastic, personal, manipulative and/or rude?

Yes ☐    No ☐

> If you answered 'yes', are you sure the others in the room would agree?

© Sandy Adirondack 2010, www.sandy-a.co.uk.
Photocopiable document. Consent required to reproduce or store electronically.

If we are discussing a matter in which I or a person connected with me (close relative, life partner, business partner etc.) has, or might have, a financial interest, or from which we might benefit, or where I or someone close to me is 'wearing two hats', do I always declare and comply with the rules on conflict of interest or conflict of loyalties?

Yes ☐    No ☐

Do I volunteer to undertake tasks for the management committee or sub-committee?

Yes ☐    No ☐

> If I volunteer, do I do what I have committed myself to?
>
> Yes ☐    No ☐
>
> If I take on something I can't do, do I notify an appropriate person in good time so alternative arrangements can be made?
>
> Yes ☐    No ☐

Do I remember at all times that I am on the management committee or sub-committee to do what is best for the organisation as a whole and all its members/users – not for me and my mates?

Yes ☐    No ☐

Do I keep confidential all sensitive information I receive as a management committee or sub-committee member, especially information about finance, personnel matters and service users?

Yes ☐    No ☐

Do I do my very best to keep up to date on matters relevant to the organisation's management, services, campaigns and other work?

Yes ☐    No ☐

When the time comes to leave the management committee or sub-committee, will I go gracefully?

Yes ☐    No ☐

**Highlight or circle the items ticked 'no' where you need to do something – starting NOW.**

© Sandy Adirondack 2010, www.sandy-a.co.uk.
Photocopiable document. Consent required to reproduce or store electronically.

# Dealing with numbers

Some people really like finance, enjoy working with figures, are really confident about what numbers mean. However, for the rest of us... !

This section aims to help you through the numbers maze. It looks at a set of management accounts and explains what the numbers mean and how you work out what they might be saying. The accounts are based on a mythical community centre, somewhat unimaginatively called Anytown Community Centre. Further information about the centre is given below.

There is also outline information on the difference between management accounts and annual accounts.

Before you read the rest of this section, it may be worth re-reading *Understanding your finances*, page 49, as it lays out the basic ground covered here.

## About Anytown Community Centre

This is a community building which runs the following range of activities from within the centre:

- a playgroup (paid for partly by a grant from BBC Children in Need, partly by subscriptions collected at the door)
- a youth cafe
- a lunch club for local older residents
- an adult reading scheme (under contract from the Anytown FE College)
- a homework club (paid for by a grant from the Anytown Charitable Trust)
- a women's health centre (under contract from the local primary care trust)
- an IT training project for long-term unemployed people (paid for by the Big Lottery Fund)

The centre is also hired out for a range of evening activities (Scouts, Brownies, indoor bowls and so on), plus parties, discos and other social functions.

It receives a core grant from Anytown Council, and encourages users and local residents to fundraise on its behalf.

On the expenditure side, costs are grouped under the following general headings:

- salaries (including those of a centre manager, a playgroup co-ordinator, a caretaker)
- running costs of the building (rent, rates, heat, light, insurance, post, telephone, photocopier)
- equipment and materials (playgroup equipment, computers, learning materials for the homework club and adult reading scheme)
- publicity, printing and stationery
- food, drink, kitchen stocks
- travel and training (including for volunteers).

## Reading management accounts

Management accounts are the regular reports that you receive which update the management committee on the organisation's financial progress in the year so far. They are generally produced monthly for larger organisations and every two to three months for smaller ones. They are based on your annual budget, and assume that it has also been broken down into monthly or quarterly estimates of income and expenditure – for more information, see *Budgeting and financial planning*, page 52.

Management accounts tend to have two main columns: 'This month' and 'Year to date'. 'This month' looks at income and expenditure for the month in question; 'Year to date' is the total for the year so far. (The accounts may also have the annual total for reference.)

Each main column is then further broken down into three parts: 'Budget', 'Actual' and 'Variance'. 'Budget' is the amount you expect to spend or receive in the month; 'Actual' is the amount you actually spent or received; 'Variance' is the difference between 'Budget' and 'Actual'.

So, for example, here are the May management accounts for Anytown Community Centre.

| | This month | | | Year to date | | | Annual total |
|---|---|---|---|---|---|---|---|
| | Actual | Budget | Variance | Actual | Budget | Variance | |
| **Income** | | | | | | | |
| 1 Playgroup | 410 | 500 | -90 | 7,260 | 7,500 | -240 | 16,000 |
| 2 Youth cafe | 340 | 400 | -60 | 1,840 | 2,000 | -160 | 4,800 |
| 3 Lunch club | 835 | 780 | 55 | 4,020 | 3,900 | 120 | 9,360 |
| 4 Reading scheme | 0 | 2,000 | -2,000 | 2,000 | 4,000 | -2,000 | 8,000 |
| 5 Homework club | 0 | 0 | 0 | 6,000 | 6,000 | 0 | 12,000 |
| 6 Women's health | 410 | 525 | -115 | 2,100 | 2,800 | -700 | 6,000 |
| 7 IT training | 6,110 | 250 | 5,860 | 12,970 | 7,250 | 5,720 | 27,000 |
| 8 Hire income | 780 | 600 | 180 | 3,680 | 3,000 | 680 | 6,000 |
| 9 Anytown Council | 10,000 | 10,000 | 0 | 10,000 | 10,000 | 0 | 20,000 |
| 10 Donations | 90 | 100 | -10 | 440 | 500 | -60 | 2,500 |
| **Total** | 18,975 | 15,155 | 3,820 | 50,310 | 46,950 | 3,360 | 111,660 |
| **Expenditure** | | | | | | | |
| 11 Salaries | 5,390 | 5,000 | 390 | 26,950 | 25,000 | 1,950 | 60,000 |
| 12 Running costs | 450 | 3,250 | -2,800 | 7,640 | 10,000 | -2,360 | 17,000 |
| 13 Equipment | 980 | 1,000 | -20 | 5,040 | 5,000 | 40 | 12,000 |
| 14 Publicity | 280 | 250 | 30 | 1,340 | 1,250 | 90 | 3,000 |
| 15 Food | 730 | 660 | 70 | 3,490 | 3,320 | 170 | 8,000 |
| 16 Travel | 90 | 160 | -70 | 510 | 830 | -320 | 2,000 |
| **Total** | 7,920 | 10,320 | -2,400 | 44,970 | 45,400 | -430 | 102,000 |

**Note:** Under income, all minus figures are worse than budget; under expenditure, all minus figures are better than budget.

## Comments

At first sight, the situation looks pretty good. The monthly income is £3,820 better than budgeted; the year to date income is £3,360 better than budgeted. The monthly expenditure is £2,400 better than budget; the year to date expenditure is also under budget, by £430. So, at first glance, all the indicators are positive.

However, you also need to look at management accounts line by line. Having done this, you may conclude that the general summary picture is a fair reflection of the overall trend. Or you may not. In this example, a careful look at the accounts will give some cause for concern. So, here goes...

## Income

1   **Playgroup**. This is £90 down on the month, and £240 down on the year to date. So, the May figure of −£90 looks to be part of a pattern, rather than just a one-off. Also, we are moving towards the summer months. Does this mean that more or fewer people will attend? In previous years, have hot summer days brought people storming into the playgroup, or have they gone to the park instead? The management committee should be concerned about the playgroup's general performance so far. Does it need to run a publicity campaign or try to encourage users to bring along other users? Should it have a 'Try four sessions for free' offer, or would this mean more lost income?

   On the positive side, the playgroup is clearly receiving its Children in Need grant on time. The year to date budget is much higher than just five times the monthly budget, which suggests that Children in Need is paying its grant (presumably of £10,000 a year) quarterly or half-yearly in advance, and everything seems to be up to date on that.

2   **Youth cafe**. Like the playgroup, this is behind both on the month and on the year to date. The management committee needs to ask similar questions to those for the playgroup. At this rate, between them the income for the playgroup and youth cafe could be down by over £1,000 by the end of the year.

3   **Lunch club**. This seems to be going well. It is slightly up on the year and on the month. Can we do anything to improve things still further?

4   **Reading scheme**. The overall income for the year is budgeted at £8,000. It seems to be coming in £2,000 chunks, so it looks as if the contract payment from the FE college is paid quarterly. We can infer that an instalment was due in May, but didn't arrive. Is that because the college is late paying or because the community centre was late invoicing? If it is simply that the payment is a week late and will come in early June rather than May, then that is nothing much to worry about. However, if the payment is going to be substantially delayed − or even not come in at all − that's a major issue. All the management committee can do is ask the questions and then decide on action, or not, according to the answers.

5   **Homework club**. Again, this seems all to be paid for by an external grant. Everything is on track. Nothing to worry about.

6   **Women's health**. Another cause for concern. Whereas the playgroup income seems to be a combination of subscriptions paid when people attend, plus an external grant, it is more likely that the

women's health centre income is all provided under contract. You can assume this for three reasons:

(a) this kind of health work is often delivered under contract from the local health authority

(b) a grant is likely to be paid quarterly rather than monthly, and it seems that the women's health project is receiving such income

(c) it would be a bit odd to have a health centre in a community centre that you had to pay to use.

Obviously, as a management committee member you would need to know (or find out) exactly where the money is coming from. If it is provided under contract it seems either that the contract payments are behind – in which case someone needs to get the invoicing sorted out – or (assuming that the health authority pays according to the number of people using the centre) that the women's health project is not attracting as many people as was hoped – in which case the end of year result is not looking at all promising.

7 **IT training**. Here the situation looks excellent. There's a major surplus on the month, and a major surplus on the year. This may be because the project is genuinely doing really well and lots more people are paying for training sessions than expected. However, it may be because the Big Lottery Fund grant has come in at the end of May rather than early June. Once again, this is something that you cannot tell from the figures alone; you have to ask questions at the management committee meeting. The role of the management accounts is to alert you to different possibilities as you go through them.

If it is indeed the case that the grant has been paid slightly earlier than anticipated (the most likely scenario), there are problems. Assuming the grant is £6,000 a quarter, which the figures would seem to suggest (as the other budgeted monthly income seems to be £250), if you take £6,000 from the May income and £6,000 from the year-to-date figures, the IT project is also behind budget.

8 **Hire income**. At last, a genuine good news story from these accounts. The income is ahead of budget both in May and for the year as a whole, so May doesn't seem to have been just a one-off good month. The question then becomes: can we do even better? Budgeting and strategic planning are not just about dealing with the bad; they are also about maximising the good.

9  **Anytown Council**. Its grant is on time. Is there any reason to assume that the second instalment will not come in on schedule? If not, no problem.

10  **Donations**. Slightly behind so far, but at this stage the amounts are pretty small. However, it seems that more is expected over the summer (the annual budget is £2,500; the budgeted income so far runs at £100 per month). Is this realistic? If not, there will be a more serious hole in income by the end of the year.

*Income summary*

The centre appears to have some problems on the income side. On current performance, despite the good results from the lunch club and hire income, it is likely that there will be an overall shortfall of around £2,000–£3,000. This is by no means disastrous, but should be enough to persuade the management committee to look again at how certain activities are run and if there are ways of raising more income from them.

## Expenditure

11  **Salaries**. Another cause for concern. They seem to be running at a steady £390 a month worse than budget. This will mean an overall deficit by the year end of nearly £5,000. It looks like a basic budgeting error (sometimes, for example, you can simply forget to allow for salary increases), but one which will have pretty serious consequences. If it continues on its current course, the salary overspend alone will wipe out around half the budgeted annual surplus.

12  **Running costs**. Again, apparently good news that probably isn't. The monthly budget of £3,250 implies that there was a major bill expected (say insurance) that either didn't arrive or wasn't paid. It looks as if the bill was expected to be £2,500–£3,000, given the budget for the month versus the actual, ongoing expenditure for the month. If so, the figures become unrepresentative of the real picture. In reality, running costs are just on budget at best. They are probably worse than budget. Things may be clearer by the end of June, especially if this bill has finally come in.

13  **Equipment**. This seems to be pretty much on budget. Given expenditure problems elsewhere, you should try to keep a pretty tight lid on this budget.

**14  Publicity**. Again, slightly over budget already. This would mean that spending money on publicity campaigns as suggested under 'Playgroup', page 114 would have to be carefully evaluated. You would need to be pretty certain of getting results.

**15  Food**. Also slightly over budget. Is this because the lunch club is going well? If so, the lunch club figures are not quite as good as they appear. Do you need to think about charging more for the lunches, because you are not making enough of a surplus on them? But would people pay if you did this?

**16  Travel**. Better than budget. Again, you may need to try to keep it this way.

*Expenditure summary*
Pretty bleak. If things continue as they are, there will probably be an overspend of at least £7,000.

## Overview

Overall, the community centre looks set to make a small loss on the year. While not disastrous, this is a cause for concern, so the management committee can expect to be facing some difficult decisions over the next few months about what is viable and where the community centre should be putting its energies. Indeed, to be really harsh, quite a few of its activities (such as the playgroup, reading scheme and IT training) are mainly financed by grant income, which by its nature is short rather than long-term. What will happen when these grants run out? Somebody may have to be doing a lot of sponsored runs to make up the shortfall!

When reading management accounts, always remember that they are just a snapshot of an organisation at a particular point in its year. Sometimes, figures that look bad may mask a pretty healthy reality; and, as with the Anytown Community Centre example, vice versa. It may even be that if you took the snapshot two weeks later the situation would look markedly different.

However, management accounts are usually a good guide to what is really going on. Study them carefully and see what you think the underlying message is. And ask whatever questions you need to satisfy yourself that you have a good grasp of the real position. It won't always be as complicated as the example given.

## Reading annual accounts

This is a difficult area for a book like this to deal with, because there are different accounting requirements according to a charity's size and set-up (for more information see *Information from the accounting system*, page 50).

Some charities have to divide their income and expenditure into 'restricted' and 'unrestricted' funds. A restricted fund is one where the donor has given money under a certain set of conditions. For example, in the Anytown Community Centre example, the BBC Children in Need grant for the playgroup would be a restricted fund because it was given specifically for the playgroup. It would be illegal to spend this money on the lunch club, for instance. However, Anytown Council's core grant can be spent on any part of the community centre's activities, and so would be deemed to be an unrestricted fund.

Charity accounts expenditure tends to be classified differently from your management accounts. Whereas Anytown Community Centre's management accounts classify expenditure under functional headings (salaries, equipment, publicity and so on), the annual accounts use more general headings such as direct charitable expenditure, fundraising and publicity costs, management and administration costs and support costs. It is basically the same information but presented in a different way.

For larger charities (and for charitable companies) there are other key differences between management accounts and annual accounts:

- Management accounts are concerned with money out and money in; annual accounts are concerned about the overall position of the charity at the year end. Annual accounts therefore include non-cash items such as an increase/decrease in the value of charity assets and investments.
- Management accounts focus on when money comes in and when it goes out; annual accounts focus on what is relevant to the year in question. So if you pay rent quarterly in advance and your final rent cheque for the year also covers some of the next year, the annual accounts will make an adjustment to reflect this (pre-payments). Conversely, if your electricity bill is paid after the financial year end but covers some of the months in the final part of that financial year, the accounts will also be adjusted accordingly (accruals).

Therefore, the year end totals on your annual accounts differ from those on your management accounts.

In general, it is best to ask your auditor, independent examiner or treasurer to take you through how your annual accounts work. It's a complicated area, and you need to understand how your charity is affected. Alternatively, read *A Practical Guide to Financial Management for Charities and Voluntary Organisations* (for details see page 130).

Either way, don't be put off by figures. Looking at management accounts is not that different from reading your own bank statement. Just as you look to see if your car insurance went through your account last month and make a mental adjustment to the final balance if it didn't, so you look at the management accounts to see what has gone in and gone out and what this means for the organisation as a whole. And then you use this information to help you decide what to do next.

# Useful addresses

## Big Lottery Fund

For details on the many regional offices see the Big Lottery Fund website: www.biglotteryfund.org.uk

For funding information or general enquiries call the BIG advice line on 0845 4 10 20 30 or email: general.enquiries@biglotteryfund.org.uk

## Charity registration and charity law

### Charity Commission

Charity Commission Direct, PO Box 1227, Liverpool L69 3UG
Tel: 0845 300 0218; email: enquiries@charitycommission.gsi.gov.uk; website: www.charity-commission.gov.uk

The Charity Commission has jurisdiction in England and Wales only.

### Charity Commission for Northern Ireland

4th Floor, 24–26 Arthur Street, Belfast, Northern Ireland, BT1 4GF
Tel: 028 9051 5490; email: admin@charitycommissionni.org.uk; website: www.charitycommissionni.org.uk

### Office of the Scottish Charity Regulator (OSCR)

2nd Floor, Quadrant House, 9 Riverside Drive, Dundee DD1 4NY
Tel: 01382 220446; email: info@oscr.org.uk; website: www.oscr.org.uk

### Her Majesty's Customs and Revenue (HMRC)

HM Revenue & Customs Charities, St Johns House, Merton Road, Liverpool L75 1BB
Tel: 0845 302 0203 (charities helpline); email: charities@hmrc.gov.uk; website: www.hmrc.gov.uk/charities

# Equal opportunities

## Equality and Human Rights Commissions

**London:** 3 More London, Riverside Tooley Street, London SE1 2RG
Tel: 020 3117 0235 (non helpline calls only);
email: info@equalityhumanrights.com

**Manchester:** Arndale House, The Arndale Centre, Manchester M4 3AQ
Tel: 0161 829 8100 (non helpline calls only);
email: info@equalityhumanrights.com

**Cardiff:** 3rd floor, 3 Callaghan Square, Cardiff CF10 5BT
Tel: 02920 447710 (non helpline calls only); textphone 029 20447713;
email: wales@equalityhumanrights.com

**Glasgow:** The Optima Building, 58 Robertson Street, Glasgow G2 8DU
Tel: 0141 228 5910 (non helpline calls only);
email: scotland@equalityhumanrights.com

**Helplines:** 0845 604 6610 (England); 0845 604 5510 (Scotland); 0845
604 8810 (Wales)

**Website:** www.equalityhumanrights.com

# Fundraising

Institute of Fundraising
Market Towers, 1 Nine Elms Lane, London SW8 5NQ
Tel: 020 7627 3436; website: www.institute-of-fundraising.org.uk

See the Institute of Fundraising website for information on fundraising codes
of practice.

# Information and training for the voluntary and community sector

## Directory of Social Change

London office: 24 Stephenson Way, London NW1 2DP
website: www.dsc.org.uk
Tel: 0845 077 7707; email: publications@dsc.org.uk or training@dsc.org.uk;
website: www.dsc.org.uk

Liverpool office: Federation House, Hope Street, Liverpool L1 9BW
Tel: 0151 708 0117; email: research@dsc.org.uk

See pages 128 to 131 for publications available from DSC.

## Local organisations

Councils for voluntary service (CVS) and rural community councils (RCCs) are registered charities that support local organisations in their area (CVS tend to work in towns and cities, RCCs in more rural areas).

For information on your local CVS, contact National Association for Voluntary and Community Action, The Tower, 2 Furnival Square, Sheffield S1 4QL
Tel: 0114 278 6636; textphone: 0114 278 7025; email: navca@navca.org.uk; website www.navca.org.uk

For information on your nearest RCC, contact: Action with Communities in Rural England (ACRE), Somerford Court, Somerford Road, Cirencester GL7 1TW
Tel: 01285 653477; email: acre@acre.org.uk; website: www.acre.org.uk

## National organisations

At the national level the national councils for voluntary service also provide help and advice.

### England

National Council for Voluntary Organisations, Regent's Wharf, 8 All Saints Street, London N1 9RL
Tel: 020 7713 6161; helpdesk: 0800 2 798 798; email: ncvo@ncvo-vol. org.uk or helpdesk@ncvo-vol.org.uk; website: www.ncvo-vol.org.uk

### Northern Ireland

Northern Ireland Council for Voluntary Action, 61 Duncairn Gardens, Belfast BT15 2GB
Tel: 028 9087 7777; email: info@nivca.org; website: www.nicva.org

### Scotland

Scottish Council for Voluntary Organisations, Mansfield Traquair Centre, 15 Mansfield Place, Edinburgh EH3 6BB
Tel: 0131 556 3882; email: enquiries@scvo.org.uk; website: www.scvo.org.uk

## Wales

Wales Council for Voluntary Action, Baltic House, Mount Stuart Square, Cardiff CF10 5FH
Tel: 0800 2888 329; email: help@wcva.org.uk; website: www.wcva.org.uk

# Investments and loans

## Charity Bank

### Headquarters

194 High Street, Tonbridge, Kent TN9 1BE
Tel: 01732 774040; email: enquiries@charitybank.org

All deposit account applications should be sent to the Tonbridge Headquarters.

### Northern office

Pannell House, 6 Queen Street, Leeds LS1 2TW
Tel: 0844 5618230; email: enquiriesnorth@charitybank.org

### London office

32–36 Loman Street, Southwark, London SE1 0EH
Tel: 01732 774040; email: enquiries@charitybank.org

If you would like to discuss a loan requirement, call the Loans Desk on 01732 774050 or email enquiries@charitybank.org

# Lotteries and gaming

Gambling Commission, Victoria Square House, Victoria Square, Birmingham B2 4BP
Tel: 0121 230 6666; email: info@gamblingcommission.gov.uk;
website: www.gamblingcommission.gov.uk

The Gambling Commission provides information about raffles, lotteries and other forms of gaming activity.

# Sources of funding

## Awards for all

Website: www.awardsforall.org.uk

For general enquiries or application forms:
Tel: 0845 4 10 20 30; textphone: 0845 039 02 04;
email: general.enquiries@awardsforall.org.uk

### England

For projects where the beneficiaries are based in the Eastern, North East, North West, South East or Yorkshire and the Humber regions:
Big Awards for All, 2 St James' Gate, Newcastle upon Tyne NE1 4BE
Tel: 0191 376 1600; textphone: 0191 376 1776

For projects where the beneficiaries are based in the East Midlands, West Midlands, London or South West regions contact:
Big Awards for All, Apex House 3 Embassy Drive Calthorpe Road Edgbaston, Birmingham B15 1TR
Tel: 0121 345 7700; minicom: 0121 345 7666

### Northern Ireland

Awards for All, 1 Cromac Quay, Cromac Wood, Ormeau Road, Belfast BT7 2JD
Tel: 028 9055 1455; textphone: 028 9055 1431;
email: enquiries.ni@awardsforall.org.uk

### Scotland

For an application pack call the hotline on 0845 600 2040.

Awards for All, 4th Floor, 1 Atlantic Quay, 1 Robertson Street, Glasgow G2 8JB
Tel: 0141 242 1400; textphone: 0141 242 1500;
scotland@awardsforall.org.uk

### Wales

Tel: 0845 4 10 20 30; textphone: 0845 6 02 16 59,
email: enquiries.wales@biglotteryfund.org.uk

# Tax and giving

## HMRC Charities

St Johns House, Merton Road, Liverpool L75 1BB
Tel: 0845 302 0203; email: charities@hmrc.gov.uk;
website: www.hmrc.gov.uk/charities

HMRC provides information and advice about the taxation of charities, including VAT.

## Charities Aid Foundation (CAF)

King's Hill, West Malling, Kent ME19 4TA
Tel: 03000 123000; email: enquiries@caf.charitynet.org;
website: www.cafonline.org

CAF provides information about tax-effective giving.

# Volunteering

## Volunteering England

Regent's Wharf, 8 All Saints Street, London N1 9RL
Tel: 0845 305 6979; email: volunteering@thecentre.org.uk;
website: www.volunteering.org.uk

Volunteering England provides advice and information on the law and best practice in volunteering.

# Publications

Charity Commission publications

The Charity Commission produces a range of free publications. The most generally useful titles include:

CC3    – The Essential Trustee: What You Need to Know
CC7    – Ex Gratia Payments by Charities
CC8    – Internal Financial Controls for Charities
CC9    – Speaking Out – Campaigning and Political Activity by Charities
CC10 – The Hallmarks of an Effective Charity
CC11 – Trustee Expenses and Payments
CC12 – Managing Financial Difficulties and Insolvency in Charities
CC14 – Investment of Charitable Funds: Basic Principles
CC15 – Charity Reporting and Accounting: The Essentials
CC18 – Use of Church Halls for Village Hall and Other Charitable Purposes
CC19 – Charities' Reserves
CC20 – Charities and Fundraising
CC21 – Registering as a Charity
CC22 – Choosing and Preparing a Governing Document
CC24 – Users on Board: Beneficiaries Who Become Trustees
CC27 – Providing Alcohol on Charity Premises
CC35 – Trustees, Trading and Tax
CC49 – Charities and Insurance
GD1    – Model Memorandum and Articles of Association for a Charitable Company
GD2    – Model Declaration of Trust for a Charitable Trust
GD3    – Model Constitution for a Charitable Unincorporated Association

Also available (online guidance):

Conflicts in your Charity
Safeguarding Children
Questions to Consider at Key Stages in the Life of a Charity
A Guide to Conflicts of Interest for Charity Trustees
Companies Act 2006

(See page 121 for contact details for the Charity Commission.)

# Publications available from DSC

The following is a selection of publications available from the Directory of Social Change (DSC), the leading publisher and provider of training for the voluntary sector. (See page 122 for contact details to request a complete list of current publications.)

## Fundraising directories

There are thousands of trusts and foundations in the UK that give grants to charities and other voluntary organisations. However, their funding criteria differ – some only give money for certain specified causes; some only give in certain geographic areas – as does the information they require from applicants. To help you identify those trusts that may fund your particular cause, the following biennial directories give detailed information, including independent commentary, on the largest UK trusts:

*The Guide to the Major Trusts, Volume 1*, DSC
*The Guide to the Major Trusts, Volume 2*, DSC

Or you can find less detailed information in:

*The Directory of Grant Making Trusts*, DSC

Information and commentary on trusts that give in specific areas of England can be found in one of the four volumes of *A Guide to Local Trusts*, covering Greater London, the Midlands, the North and the South of England (DSC) or DSC's subscription website www.companygiving.org.uk.

For information on Wales, see DSC's subscription website www.trustfunding.org.uk

If you are trying to raise money or other support from the corporate sector, you can refer to *The Guide to UK Company Giving* (DSC).

There are specialist fundraising guides available including:

*Environment Funding Guide*, Denise Lillya, DSC, 2010
*Government Funding Guide*, Sarah Johnston, DSC, 2010
*Sports Funding Guide*, Tom Traynor and Denise Lillya, DSC, 2009
*Youth Funding Guide*, Denise Lillya, DSC, 2009

If you are trying to raise money from local, regional, national or European government sources see DSC's subscription website www.governmentfunding.org.uk

## Fundraising handbooks

A popular title that provides detailed practical advice on all aspects of fundraising for charity is:

*The Complete Fundraising Handbook*, 5th edition, Nina Botting Herbst and Michael Norton, DSC in association with the Institute of Fundraising, 2007

For information on how to approach funders:

*Finding Company Sponsors for Good Causes*, Chris Wells, DSC, 2000,

To help you put together effective applications for support:

*Writing Better Fundraising Applications*, 4th edition, Mike Eastwood and Michael Norton, DSC, 2010

Once you have secured your donors, advice on how to develop your links with them is given in:

*Looking after your Donors*, Karen Gilchrist, DSC, 2000

Details of how to plan and organise different types of fundraising events are provided by these books:

*Complete Special Events Handbook*, Pauline Carter, DSC, 2009
*Tried and Tested Ideas for Local Fundraising Events,* 3rd edition, Sarah Passingham, DSC, 2003

## Management

The standard guide for managers of small and medium-sized voluntary organisations:

*Just About Managing?*, 4th edition, Sandy Adirondack, London Voluntary Service Council, 2005

An essential guide to leading, managing and governing nonprofit organisations:

*Managing Without Profit*, Mike Hudson, DSC, 2009

A practical approach to business planning in the voluntary sector:

*The Complete Guide to Business and Strategic Planning for Voluntary Organisations*, Alan Lawrie, 3rd edition, DSC, 2007

Aspects of people-management are covered in:

*Essential Volunteer Management*, 2nd edition, Steve McCurley and Rick Lynch, DSC, 1998, reprinted with updates, 2007
*Keeping Volunteers*, Steve McCurley and Rick Lynch, DSC, updated reprint 2010
*Recruiting Volunteers*, Fraser Dyer & Ursula Jost, DSC, updated reprint 2010

## Communication

Every voluntary organisation needs to put its message across effectively. The following titles all provide you with helpful, practical advice:

*Media Relations* (Speed Read), Moi Ali, DSC, 2009
*Writing for the Web* (Speed Read), Moi Ali, DSC, 2009
*How to Produce Inspiring Annual Reports: A Guide for Voluntary, Arts and Campaigning Organisations*, Ken Burnett and Karin Weatherup, DSC, 2000

## Finance

Don't let figures frighten you. If you have been asked to be treasurer of a voluntary group, or simply want a good grounding in how charity finances work, try:

*The Charity Treasurer's Handbook*, 3rd edition, Gareth Morgan, DSC, 2010

If you are looking for information on more specific financial areas, these two books will guide you through what you need to know:

*A Practical Guide to Financial Management for Charities and Voluntary Organisations*, 3rd edition, Kate Sayer, DSC in association with Sayer Vincent, 2007
*A Practical Guide to VAT for Charities and Voluntary Organisations*, 3rd edition, Kate Sayer & Alastair Hardman, DSC in association with Sayer Vincent, 2008

# Law

The key introductory guide to what is a charity, and what constitutes charitable activity, is:

*Charitable Status: A Practical Handbook*, 6th edition, Justin Blake, DSC, 2008

You can find information on the law as it affects charities, community groups and other voluntary organisations in:

*The Russell-Cooke Voluntary Sector Legal Handbook*, 3rd edition, James Sinclair Taylor and the Charity Team and Russell-Cooke, Editor: Sandy Adirondack, DSC, 2009

*Voluntary but not Amateur*, 8th edition, Ruth Hayes and Jacki Reason, DSC in association with Bates, Wells & Braithwaite, 2009

Details of specific topics are provided in:

*Charitable Incorporated Organisations*, Gareth Morgan, DSC, 2012

*Data Protection for Voluntary Organisations*, 3rd edition, Paul Ticher, DSC, 2009

*Flexible Working* (Speed Read), Yvonne Perry, DSC, 2010

*Age Discrimination* (Speed Read), Yvonne Perry, DSC, 2010

*Minute Taking*, Lee Comer and Paul Ticher, DSC, 2012

# Index

accountability 4, 23, 27, 67–72, 98, 104; to funders 69–70; to staff 70–1; to users 70

accounts/accounting 24, 49–55, 57, 67, 69, 84, 107, 111; accruals basis 50–1, 118; annual 118–19; management 7, 50, 54, 55, 111–19 passim; SORP 50–1

advice/advisers 7–9 passim, 27, 45, 85, 94

age, of trustee 11

agenda, meetings of trustees 76–8, 81, 83, 102, 109; dyslexia 78

aims 5, 30–4 passim, 68, 69 see also priorities

appeals 63

appraisals, staff 24, 43–4; 360 degree system 44

approaches, to donors 62

assets 7, 49, 54, 57, 64–5, 118; register 64, 107

association, memorandum of 98

audits/auditors 49–51, 84, 107; committee 85

Awards for All 60, 125

balance sheet 49, 50

bankrupt, undischarged 11

BBC Children in Need 60

beneficiaries 6, 9, 12–13, 27, 29, 30, 69, 70

BIG Lottery Fund 58, 60, 69, 121

borrowing 8

briefing 85, 86, 88

budgets 7, 24, 32, 49, 52–4, 61, 81, 83, 106, 112

campaigns 100

Cancer Research UK 4, 31

care, acting with 7, 8, 27

cash 7, 24, 65, 83, 106; flow 52–4 passim

chair, of sub-committee 89; of trustees 44–5, 71, 75, 77, 79–83 passim, 102

charges, to users 52

charitable incorporated organisation 98, 107

charitable status 55, 98; Handbook 3, 131

Charities Act (1993) 11; (2006) 9

Charities Aid Foundation 126

Charity Bank 65, 124

Charity Commission 4, 8, 9, 11, 26–7, 50, 51, 58, 67, 83, 84, 98, 108, 121; for Northern Ireland 121; publications 127

checklists 97–105

cheques, signing 24, 54–5, 81, 106

chief executive/director 8, 23, 41, 44–5, 70, 81, 89, 104

child protection policy 48

collaboration with other organisations 30, 31, 37

commitment 26, 36, 75; financial 24

communication 71–2, 130; internal 25, 44, 46, 48, 71, 88–9, 102

companies 60–1; limited 98, 107; registered 8

compensation, for lost earnings 9

confidence 17, 29, 77; donors' 36

confidentiality 67, 72, 75, 110

confusion 85, 86, 88

constitution 4, 5, 8, 19, 23, 30, 54, 65, 67, 75, 76, 82, 98, 107

consultants/consultation 27, 100, 104

contacts 12, 13, 59–62 passim

contracts 3, 6, 8, 27, 61, 104

contribution 12–13, 17, 20

conviction 11

costs 52–4 passim, 57, 61, 71, 112, 116, 118

councils for voluntary service 45, 60, 61, 94, 123–4

criticism, constructive 46

data protection 99

debts 7, 8

decisions 46, 47, 71, 79–82 passim, 88, 98; -making 5, 6, 11, 23, 26, 29, 39, 75–6, 80, 87, 88, 102; ratification 88

deficits 49, 51

definition, of trustee 3–9, 20

delegating 24, 33, 34, 62, 67, 76, 85–9, 94

development 53; staff 41–4 passim, 87

directories 61, 128

Directory of Social Change 31, 45, 122–3; publications 128–31

disability 42, 45; Discrimination Act 32

discipline, staff 45, 104; Acas Code 45

discrimination 45

dismissal 45

disqualification 11; Company Directors – Act (1986) 11

donors/funders 27, 36, 57–64 passim, 67, 69–70

duration, of committees 88; of trustee service 19–20

effectiveness, personal 93, 97, 109–10
email 71–2
employment 43, 45; conditions of 87,
   103; contract 45, 99, 103; law 41, 43
equal opportunities 38, 42, 48, 87, 99,
   103, 122
Equality and Human Rights
   Commission 122
equipment 25, 35, 64
Essential Trustee, The 98
expenditure 49, 52, 54, 106, 112–13,
   116–18 passim
expenses 9, 95
experience 12, 13, 26, 93

feedback 46, 47, 70
finance 4, 7–8, 24–5, 49–55, 68, 83–5,
   99, 106–7, 111–19; committee 55, 85;
   publications 130
flexibility, employment 42, 43
following through 95
fraud 7, 8, 83, 106
fundraising 51, 57–66, 99; committee 62,
   63, 86; directories 128; ethics of 58;
   handbooks 129; Institute 122

Gambling Commission 124
getting most from trusteeship 93–6
Gift Aid 63
governance 5, 33, 44, 65, 71, 94
grants 35, 36, 51, 53, 55, 118
grievances 45, 104

health and safety 33, 45, 48, 53, 64, 99,
   103
history 36–7
HM Revenue and Customs 45, 63, 121;
   Charities 126
honorarium 9

impact 69, 70
income 4, 28, 49, 50, 52, 54, 60–1, 106,
   112–16, 118
incorporation 8, 107
independence 28
induction, staff 24, 42, 104; pack 99
industrial and provident society 98, 107
information 5, 13, 26, 94, 102
insurance 8, 64, 65, 99, 108; employer's
   liability 45; national 45, 55
interest, conflicts of 6, 100, 110;
   declaration of 6; donor 62; register
   of 100
intimidation 78
investment 24, 50, 65, 107, 118, 124
involvement 36; staff 34; volunteers 12,
   34, 47; users 34

jargon 64
job descriptions 42, 43, 46, 88, 103;
   vacancies 42

keeping in touch 94

law/legislation 8, 26–7, 35, 45, 52, 57, 63,
   68, 83, 99, 103; employment 41, 43,
   45, 103; publications 131; Russell-Cooke
   Handbook 45; and volunteers 48
liabilities 4, 6–8 passim, 49, 93
local authority 6, 69

management 4, 5, 12, 24–6, 44, 65, 71,
   89, 98; committee 4–6, 23–8, 30–8
   passim, 41, 43, 45, 62, 63, 66–71,
   75–85 passim, 87, 89, 93, 94, 97–101
   passim, 103, 106–10 passim;
   publications 129–30
managers 41, 43
meetings, AGM 11, 71, 83; chief
   executive and chair 45; management
   committee 11–12, 26, 75–80, 95, 102,
   109; open 69; preparation for 11, 95,
   109; sub-committee 88, 102
members 27, 29, 67, 71, 87, 98
minutes, of meetings 6, 11, 77–9 passim,
   82, 95, 99, 102
mission 5, 68; statement 23, 30–1, 33, 34
monitoring 5, 7, 23, 24, 34, 42, 52, 57,
   70, 76, 87
motivation 4, 19–20; volunteers 12, 47

National Lottery 60 see also BIG
needs 29, 34, 70, 94
negativity 79
newsletters 71
nit-picking 79

objects 8, 23, 30, 47, 54, 68, 75, 100
obligations, legal 52, 57, 83
Office of Scottish Charity Regulator 121
opposition 6, 78, 79, 82

partnerships 35, 37, 104
pay, of staff 43–5 passim, 55; of
   trustee 8–9
penalties 41, 45
performance, staff 43–4
photos/pictures/pie charts 68, 69
plans/planning 5, 23, 24, 35–6, 52, 65, 75;
   financial 24, 49, 52–4, 61–2, 70;
   SPOTS 36; strategic 34–6, 61, 100
policies 5, 38, 75
post, opening 7
powers 7, 67, 87, 88
press/media coverage 69

principles 38, 58
priorities 5, 34, 75, 95
problems 34, 76, 87; financial 51, 53
procedures 38; proceduralism 79
projects 59; committee 86
promotion, staff 42
property/premises 25, 37, 42, 64, 99
prudence 7, 8, 27
publications 99, 127–31
publicity 25, 70, 99
purposes, of managing committee 77; of
    organisation 8, 23, 30–1; of sub-
    committees 88

questions, asking 27, 94

race 45, 87
reasons to be trustee 15
recklessness 79
records 49, 54, 64, 65, 83
recruitment 87; staff 24, 42, 46, 52, 81,
    87, 103; volunteers 46, 47, 87, 103 '
redundancy, staff 53
refusing to be trustee 17
relationships 58–9, 64
removal from trusteeship 11
reports/reporting 7, 34, 68, 70, 83, 88,
    89, 101, 106; annual 67–9
reputation 9, 25–6
requirements, legal 8, 11, 41, 69;
    practical 11–13, 51, 67
reserves 51–3 passim, 107
resignation 11
resources 3–4, 25, 34, 35, 57–66
responsibilities 3–8 passim, 24, 45, 55, 57,
    75, 84, 85, 93, 95, 99; personal 6
restricted funds 118
results 33, 35, 36
retainer 9
reviews 43, 44, 68–9, 95, 100
risk 7, 65, 83, 89, 93, 100, 106
roles 23–72 passim; management
    committee 23–8; of volunteers 46–8
rules 78; makers 27
rural community councils 123
rushing 78

Samaritans 30
secretary, of management committee 78,
    82–3
selection 87; staff 24, 42, 87;
    volunteers 47, 87
selling 61

size, of management committee 77
skills 12, 15, 26, 42, 46, 93
sponsorship 61
staff 3, 5, 8–9, 24, 25, 27, 30, 33–8
    passim, 41–6, 48, 52, 62, 67, 68, 70–1,
    85–7 passim, 89, 94, 101, 103;
    attending trustee meetings 8–9, 80;
    committee 86; make-up 42; relations
    with 41, 46, 48, 80
steering committee 70
stock 65, 107
straplines 31
sub-committees 24, 27, 33, 43, 45, 48,
    55, 62, 70, 76, 85–6, 88, 94, 98–101
    passim, 103
success 34–6 passim, 44, 64
supervision, staff 24, 42, 44–5, 71, 81, 99;
    volunteers 47
surplus 3, 24, 49, 51

targets 33–4, 43–4, 69; SMART 33
tasks 33, 34, 89
tax 45, 55, 63, 67
termination, of service 110
terms of reference 88; of service 19–20
time, devotion of 9,11, 17, 93, 95, 96
title 4–5
training 9; management committee 99,
    107; staff/volunteers 42–4 passim, 47,
    103, 104
treasurer 24, 51, 52, 55, 83–5, 106
trust 44; breach of 7
trust deed 98
trusts, grant-making 60

users 12–13, 25, 27, 29, 30, 34–7 passim,
    52, 70, 87, 99, 100

values 38, 94, 100
vision 29–30, 34
visits 37, 70, 94
Volunteering England 126
volunteers 3, 4, 12, 17, 24, 25, 27, 30,
    33–8 passim, 46–8, 67, 70–1, 85, 87,
    94, 99, 101, 103, 104; code of
    practice 47; and law 47; National
    Centre for 48
voting rights 98

weaknesses 37
websites 71–2
working groups 85–7, 94
working practices 42, 43